Any Chance of a Game?

Barney Ronay is 30 and lives in London. He writes for *When Saturday Comes* and the *Guardian*. He is the co-editor of the *WSC Companion to Football* and creator of the mildly amusing satirical sporting website *The Pitch*. He plays right back.

Any Chance of a Game?

A season at the ugly end of park football

Barney Ronay

EBURY
PRESS

Thanks to Andrew Goodfellow and Paul Moreton.
Thanks also to *When Saturday Comes*.

For Kate

Contents

1 3 5 7 9 10 8 6 4 2

First published 2005 by Ebury Press,
An imprint of Random House,
20 Vauxhall Bridge Road, London SW1V 2SA

Random House Australia (Pty) Limited
20 Alfred Street, Milsons Point, Sydney,
New South Wales 2061, Australia

Random House New Zealand Limited
18 Poland Road, Glenfield, Auckland 10, New Zealand

Random House South Africa (Pty) Limited
Endulini, 5a Jubilee Road, Parktown 2193, South Africa

The Random House Group Limited Reg. No. 954009

www.randomhouse.co.uk

Printed and bound in Great Britain by Mackays of Chatham plc, Kent

A CIP catalogue record for this book
is available from the British Library.

Cover designed by gray318
Typeset by seagulls

ISBN 0 09190028X

Warming up

You always know when it's Friday. Friday has something about it right from the moment you wake up. It's the same with every other day of the week. They all have their own distinct feel. Monday is just Monday morning all day. Tuesday is hard work all around. Important things happen on Wednesday; it's a grown-up kind of day. Thursday feels like now we're really starting to get somewhere. And Friday is special. There's no other day quite like it.

"Cheers," Dan says, taking his drink. "What's this?"

"Peanuts."

"Salted. I said dry roasted."

"Yeah, well I don't like dry roasted. The dust at the bottom of the bag feels like it's dissolving your mouth. What's it meant to taste of anyway?"

"The dust," Dan says, raising his glass, "is the whole point."

But the best thing about Friday is Friday night. That first drink of the evening, I don't just want to drink it. I want to eat it. I want to get inside the glass and swim in it. Not that it usually lasts very long. It's like what someone once said about drinking. Getting drunk is great. Those first few minutes are as good as it gets. *Being* drunk, on the other hand, isn't always quite as much fun.

"As soon as he leaves I'm going over there," Dan says, eyeing the fruit machine.

"It's too crowded. You'll never make it."

"The same bloke has been feeding the same machine all night. It's ready to pay out."

"Before you go, just tell me why you're dressed like that."

"Dress-down Friday," he shrugs.

"You look like Prince William."

"New rules," Dan says, looking over my shoulder at a group of about fifteen women who've just arrived at the far end of the bar. "No jean-cut slacks allowed. These are chino-cut."

We're standing in a corner of the Itinerant Goat, a new pub with wooden floors and rows of champagne bottles behind the bar. Next to us a circle of fat-necked men in stripy shirts are laughing slightly too loudly. They look ready for a big night out, one that has started already at 6.30, with the light fading outside and the beery glow from the lamps near the ceiling only just starting to take over.

Looming at least a head taller than most of the crowd, a familiar figure has appeared by the door and started to work his way towards us. Simon has his long coat buttoned all the way up to his neck and a bag strapped across his shoulders. The only thing the Itinerant Goat really has going for it is that it's the nearest pub to where we all work.

"Drink?" he shouts when he gets close enough. We hold up our empty glasses and he turns towards the scrum at the bar.

"That's better," he says when he's finally made it across, and after he's spent a few moments trying to get most of his pint glass actually inside his head.

"I spoke to Keith today," he adds.

"That's nice for you."

"He said we're at home to Parsons Green on Sunday. They're good. Fifth in the table. And we've only got ten so far."

"Not again. What is wrong with people?"

"Keith told me he's got this idea for a reality TV show. It's like the reverse of Sunday football. You get Premiership footballers to spend a day doing a Sunday player's week-day job, but only something really difficult. Roy Keane organising a conference in Frankfurt. Michael Owen teaching Japanese."

"That's his idea?"

"He said it's genius."

"Would you like to help fight against animal experiments?"

A middle-aged woman with immaculate blonde hair has appeared out of the crowd. She shakes a tin at us. She seems to be actually expecting an answer.

"Er. All right then," I say, fumbling for some change.

"Thanking you so much."

She turns to Simon and stares at him until he gives in and finds some coins. Only Dan doesn't flinch and soon she's moved on to the circle of crew cuts next to us.

"Always seems a bit weird. Collecting in a pub."

"They know people are going to feel guilty," Simon mutters.

"I think it's a bit out of order," Dan says. "You come in here to forget about everything. Not to get chased around by equal rights for dogs."

"I meant normal people," Simon says, but I'm not really listening as I spot another familiar face near the bar.

Laura has started to nudge her way through the crush of bodies towards our end of the room. It's always weird seeing a familiar face in a crowd of strangers. She's dressed smartly, her brown hair tied back with just a single strand falling across her face, and I keep watching, waiting for the moment she looks up and finally sees us. The thick-necked blokes part respectfully to let her through.

"You could have found a darker corner to hide in," she says, squeezing my arm.

"Yeah. But then you might have found us hours ago."

"Don't listen to him," Dan says, kissing her cheek. "He's a very rude man. It's my round."

"White wine spritzer."

"Ha ha. Make sure you say, 'for the lady'."

It's dark in the street now and around us everything has suddenly become much noisier. It feels like people are settling in for the night. Food on giant plates is ferried past by men in white aprons.

"I bought a wedding present for Dick and Liz," Laura is saying.

"This is something I don't get," Dan says.

"You're not getting married."

"Funny. Wedding presents, though. It always seems a bit

much after everything else. They're getting married, so I have to buy them a pot. Why?"

"It's friendly."

"Turning up is friendly. Taking a weekend out of your summer is friendly. Spending five hundred quid on a stag do is friendly. They want a frying pan at the end of all that?"

"So what you're saying is you're basically just so happy for them."

The bar is completely full now. There's a kind of steam hanging over the middle of the room. A woman in a short skirt stands up on a bench and dances. Someone cheers. A glass smashes nearby. And without any of us even starting it, without any help at all, the talk has turned to football.

"My knee is still killing me from last week," Simon says. "I think it's the hard ground. Mud suits me."

"Did you see Nev? I swear he was having a heart attack. He tried to talk to me after their third goal and no words came out. Nothing at all."

Already I'm starting to feel a bit uncomfortable, glancing around at Laura, who's smiling and looking as though she's listening, even though there's nothing she can add to any of this; and even though I know for a fact she finds it pretty boring.

"We'd better go in a minute," I say, draining the froth at the bottom of my glass.

"Are you sure?" Laura asks, but it's the right moment to leave. Simon has started yawning. Dan has been talking on his phone to someone called Belinda for the last couple of minutes and I can feel one of his sudden disappearing acts about to come on.

"All right then. See you Sunday," Simon says.

"Yeah. See you then."

"I won't," Laura says, buttoning her coat.

"You can if you like," Dan says. "You know you're always invited."

"Tempting of course. But no thanks."

"Sunday then."

"Sunday."

And then we're off out into the cold air. A narrow lane funnels us all the way down to Liverpool Street and the clearing house of Tubes and trains and cabs that will take us west towards home.

Friday hasn't quite stopped feeling like Friday yet, but it's definitely become a gateway towards something else. The jamboree of Saturday morning. The excitement of Saturday night. And then Sunday when the week ends and begins again all at the same time. A part of me has already started counting it down.

1
Sunday morning

Sunday September 6th 2004
Bolingbroke Athletic vs. Parsons Green FC

Professional footballers are fond of saying that there are no easy games any more. Which just goes to show (a) that they've never played in the South West London Sunday Morning League; and (b) that they've never played us.

Not that we're much worse than anyone else you might come across on a Sunday morning. In fact Bolingbroke Athletic Football Club has a proud record. We've been in existence for five years; five full seasons of warm Septembers, mid-winter trench warfare and clear skies in May. Today will be our fifth game of the season. After two months of gentle dress rehearsal, it feels as though the season has finally begun. The air is fresher this morning and the trees are almost bare by the side of the road.

Awash with scrambled eggs and coffee, gargling vitamin pills and sherbet lemon painkillers, I'm driving south along five miles of banks and supermarkets and fast food joints looking peaky in the lilac morning light. The streets are always empty at this time on a Sunday. The route to the ground is so familiar I can follow it without thinking.

I picked Dan up in Clapham. When he answered the door

he didn't look just half asleep, he looked half alive. Pouchy-eyed and unshaven, he got into the car without saying a word. He still hasn't said anything. He's wearing a pair of tracksuit bottoms that look like they've been trimmed across the bottom of each leg with a blunt knife. His jacket is zipped right up to the neck and his fair hair is sticking up in prickly clumps.

"What did you do last night?"

"The usual. Pub. Club. Home."

"Who was there?"

"Simon. Keith. That lot. I was really ... really wasted."

He coughs painstakingly. When he stops his face has been almost completely drained of colour.

"We met these girls in Zeus. One of them came back to my place." He takes a deep breath. "She was this really sexy nurse."

"Sounds all right. Jesus look at that. Buses are the worst."

"It was all right at first," he says, closing his eyes. "The thing is, it turned out she's assistant head of derivatives and junk bond trading at Godby Samson Bach. She was only dressed as a really sexy nurse. They were on a hen night."

"Easy mistake to make."

"We ended up having a massive argument about the investment potential of new technology-driven hedge fund portfolios."

Dan works for a bank in the City. I'm not sure exactly what he does there. To be honest, I've never been that keen to narrow it down too precisely.

"Probably not what you had in mind then."

"I spent the night on my own sofa. She still wouldn't talk to me at breakfast. It was like being married. No offence."

"None taken. I'm not married."

"Yeah, well. You know. What were you doing anyway? Watching *Gardeners' Question Time?*"

"I think you mean *Gardeners' World. Gardeners' Question Time* is a radio programme, so you couldn't technically watch it. That would be impossible."

"Whatever. Dick."

On the map our home ground at Halfmarshes looks tiny, a smear of lime green with a faint rectangle indicating a pitch. It's lodged in the sprawl of winding roads that spread south from Wandsworth Common towards Tooting, a no-man's-land of pebbledash and deserted one-way streets. We're getting closer now and I'm starting to feel really awake for the first time. Thirsty, a bit sick, and with a deep and lingering ache in both knees, but definitely awake.

Halfmarshes isn't much of a home. The little road that leads down to it appears suddenly between two houses, a single lane set back from the street that gives a glimpse, between trees, of an expanse of green. There's a small car park and a row of huts to one side with a room for the home and away teams and a row of showers at the back. Apart from the benches and some creaking hot water pipes, it's basically a park toilet with a padlock.

The two pitches slope down towards the trees and the railway line at the far end. People walk their dogs here during the week and there are parts where you have to watch where you tread. Keith calls it the San Shiteo. But you can get used to anywhere.

Today there's something in the air that isn't quite winter yet, a smell of live grass and warm mud after the heavy rain of the last few weeks. Dan is smoking his first cigarette of the morning as we walk across towards the changing rooms. Inside, the air is already thick with clean kit and the dusty heat of the radiator.

"All right, lads?" Keith shouts across the room.

"Keith."

"Keith."

Keith has thick black hair and a low, dark brow. His white Bolingbroke shirt is stretched tight across his shoulders. Keith is almost completely square, five feet six in all directions. He has all the qualifications required to be team captain: he always turns up and he has by far the loudest voice.

As a player Keith is from the school of last ditch desperate defending. His game is based around sudden acts of violence. It still surprises me how little it takes to get him going. Before you've even had a touch of the ball he's already goggle-eyed with rage and on his third foul of the game.

Most of the team are already here. We're a fairly typical bunch, I suppose. Although it probably always seems that way when you've been playing with the same people for the last five years. If I had to describe us I'd probably do it like this:

Lars

Goalkeeper and hypochondriac.
You might think that you've got a bad back.
His is much worse.

Me

No pace, no tackling before 10.30 and no breakfast this morning. Hanging on at right back.

Keith

Limitless energy combined with extremely limited talent. Defence, yellow cards and captain.

Nev

Age uncertain. Usually seen either naked or eating early lunch. Enthusiasm almost makes up for near immobility. Heavyweight central defence.

Dave

Two kids and a Volvo estate. Looks like he's enjoying himself. What's he doing here? Left back and lifts to away games.

Jerome

Younger, fitter, hard to understand what he's doing hanging around here with the rest of us. Showboating right midfield.

Dan

My best mate. Although sometimes I do wonder why. Don't leave him alone with your fags, lunch or girlfriend. Central midfield.

Charlie

Lives with his mum. Suspected of collecting ornamental World War Two soldiers. Possibly building bomb in garden shed. Central midfield.

Lucien

Token Goth. Quick, skilful, wears mascara. Left midfield.

Simon

Pointlessly tall. Ever present for the last five years. Proof that sometimes nice guys also come last. Gangling target man.

Bob

Older than your dad. Maybe older than your grandad. Wears gloves and scarf. Still plays in black and white. Wily centre forward.

I sit down in the corner next to Jerome and start unpacking my boots, which are flaked with mud and still a little damp from last week.

"Mr B. How's it?"

"It's all right."

Jerome has left a neatly folded pile of clothes on the bench. He's standing up to tuck his thin gold chain inside a white vest. I notice this week he's got a tiny tramline shaved into his eyebrow.

"Keith said you might not come this week. We need you, Mr B. Don't leave us."

"What happened to your face? Have you been fighting again?"

Actually, I have been thinking about missing a week or two. I don't remember telling Keith about it though. Skipping games never goes down that well.

"Here he is. Jesus Christ. The state of him."

Keith has got his arm around the figure in the doorway, gripping his thin white neck in a headlock. Lucien, our left winger, is a member of that surprisingly common breed, the footballing Goth. His hair hangs in a jagged fringe as he tries to shake himself free. He's wearing all black and carrying his kit in a spiked rubber bag.

"Keith, fuck off. I don't feel like it today. And no, I'm not."

"Not what?"

"Jesus Christ."

The strangest thing about Lucien is that on the pitch he's a natural: fast and low to the ground, with the neat movements of the born footballer. That's the thing about footballing goths. Often they're your best player.

We're all changed now, except for Nev, our centre half, who comes wandering in from the showers still completely naked. Every team I've played in has someone like Nev. Before you've even put your bag down or switched on the lights, some Sunday morning exhibitionist will be padding around in the nude, debating the merits of the new Ford Focus like he's at home in his own bathroom. With Nev it might have something to do with the tight fit of our scratchy nylon shirts across his enormous belly and his cannonball head with its many chins. In real life Nev runs a catering company and he's got four kids and a wife with very expensive tastes in foreign holidays. Last season his thin and very serious-looking teenage son, Marcus, played for us a few times.

"All right, lads. Feeling a bit rough this morning, are we? Out pulling the birds last night?"

"Er, not really."

"Saturday night on the lagers. I'll have to join you one of these days. Show you how it's done."

"Yeah. That would be great, Nev."

Dan seems to have found something on his boot that he needs to study very closely. Another thing Nev manages to do is to sound every week more like the impression we do of him when he's not there.

Perhaps it's the smell, or the full-frontal nudity, or maybe the pink tinge of sun above the trees above the far end of the field, but this morning I'm desperate to get outside. This is my favourite part of the day. The ground is still wet with dew and I can't stop myself sprinting after the clean white ball as it fizzes away, bouncing in deep green footprints towards the near goal, which gleams with a halo of low white sun.

In the goalmouth I stand next to Lars, our gangling goalkeeper. He's wearing a bright yellow goalie's jersey and padded black trousers and he's stretching his left leg gingerly.

"I've still got that hamstring," he says, shaking his head. "It's done something to my knee."

Do tall people complain more than short people? Maybe they just have a lower pain threshold. Lars is six feet four. He practically glows with health.

"I really shouldn't be here at all. I can't take goal kicks. Keith will have to do it."

"Maybe you should start doing yoga. Like Dave."

"Not with my back."

Dave, skinny with a shaggy haircut, is doing some kind of t'ai chi-style stretching routine near the corner flag. Dave is slightly older than me. He doesn't look like a footballer. For the first half of a game he's usually fairly anonymous. What Dave has is a wiry stamina, the long-distance runner's gait that sees him trotting forward determinedly in the second half just as everyone else is starting to fade.

"Oi, check it out." Jerome tugs at my sleeve. He's laughing at Charlie as he tries to organise a warm-up in the far goal. Short-legged and sergeant-majorly, Charlie is our midfield general. He does a lot of pointing. He's pointing at Dan right now. Dan ignores him, pausing only to smash a loose ball into the roof of the empty net from five yards.

"Just one of you on the goal. Groups of two or three the rest. Let's be warm and ready for this. No, one of you on the keeper ..."

It's impossible to tell the standard of football you're about to witness from the quality of the pre-match warm-up. I've seen Sunday teams go through minutely rehearsed drills only to perform like a sulky fifth XI when the game kicks off. On the other hand when I was thirteen I went to watch England play at Wembley and saw John Barnes and Chris Waddle – two of the most skilful players of their generation – warm up by hitting long passes to each other across the pitch, creeping closer to the head of the baton-twirling Grenadier Guard who led the marching band. Eventually Waddle hit him, knocking his bearskin helmet over his eyes. Waddle gave the crowd a thumbs-up and trotted off to pose for some pictures. Compared to Barnes and Waddle the Bolingbroke warm-up is a professional affair. Well-meaning stretching exercises mingle with spectacular punts towards goal and attempts at bicycle kicks that disappear towards the corner flag. No Sunday league warm-up is complete without somebody taking a ball out to the touchline and sending in crosses, a cue for the entire team to pile into the six-yard box and attempt to backheel at least four or five different balls into the net at the same time. What this is supposed to be preparation for, I've yet to work out.

Charlie has given up by now and is marching across to say something to Bob, our centre forward. Bald, pot-bellied and capable of small-scale flashes of brilliance, Bob is also well advanced into early middle age. He tends to spend just a few moments in each game showcasing his one-man band talents. Put the ball on a plate for him and every now and then you'll catch a glimpse of the younger Bob, the one who moved in almost the same way, just much quicker. The fact remains though: Bob has played up front in every game last season without scoring a single goal. He's going through a stretching routine that involves bending very slightly at the waist and reaching a hand in the direction of his knees.

We line up for kick-off and I look at the opposition for the first time. From a distance all teams look the same, a collection of figures yet to separate out into recognisable types. You make the calculations of weight, height and speed. You look for weak links and familiar giveaways. Just for a moment football feels a bit like fighting.

Today there are no obvious signs of weakness in the opposition, no pale camel-like figures fretting in the unaccustomed strip. You get a good idea from the boots (worn in?), the amount of faded white strapping on knees (sign of the seasoned player), and even from the nicknames. Beware of the bantering team. This lot look as though they've shared the same playground, clubhouse, family Christmases and shrinking gene pool for the last thirty years. Proper pub teams are rare these days. When you do meet one you know you're going to get a game.

Simon comes across and hits me between the shoulder blades. Squaring up, we face each other.

"Yes. Come on."

"Give it some."

I jump towards him and bounce off his chest in the style of American footballers before a huddle. This is our pre-match warm-up. It started off as a joke a long time ago. I'm not really sure what it is now.

The referee is short and dapper with a silvery quiff and a prominent stomach. He gives a short speech on playing fair, not swearing and his personal interpretation of the new FIFA offside directive ("I don't understand it"). The sky has closed in. As Charlie kicks us off it feels low above our heads, a warm white canopy. The ball is played long and high and eventually out of play into the bushes on the far left-hand side.

"Straight in. Switched on."

"Big first ten, whites."

"Let's have it. Big head on this."

The ball is shuttled backwards from Charlie to Dan and then across to me at right back. Sometimes at the beginning of a game the ball feels slightly unreal. It's easily floated around, not yet programmed with neurotic purpose. We're all feeling our way into this, convincing ourselves that we can still make the weekly leap of faith.

At this point it's worth getting something out of the way. Am I any good at football? Even now I'm not completely sure. At moments like these it really could go either way. A nice first touch, a tackle and a pass, and suddenly the automatic responses all fall into place. And, yes, I'm not bad.

But am I any *good*? Sometimes I think this is why we play. None of us is really sure. You play to test your limits and to nurture that image of yourself, kept in deep storage somewhere, as a proper footballer. If I had to define my style of play, I'd file myself under frustrating maverick, promising under-achiever. A childhood spent kicking a ball around has equipped me with a range of basic skills that still come very easily, only slightly dulled by age and by twenty years of park pitch football. So basically, yes, I'm not bad. Pretty average most of the time. But every now and then, you know, if the ball drops right... Really, you should have seen me last week. Oh, never mind.

The first few minutes of the game see us meandering upfield. There's no other game on the pitch next to us this morning. We're out here alone, a collection of coloured shapes in the middle of half a mile of grass. We win a throw-in on the right-hand side. This is my part of the pitch, so I have another early touch, enough to suggest that my ankles, lungs and self-esteem might yet make it through the morning. Dan jumps into a tackle and slips the ball back to me.

"Barn."

"Barn, mate."

"Barn, fucking send it."

This has always happened to me in teams. I get abbreviated. *Barn: man on. Barn's ball. Barn, what the FUCK was that?* My name just isn't a football name. You're expected to shout it out when you want the ball. "John's ball!" "Dave's up!" These are all fine. But "Barn's ball" is too difficult to say. And "Barney's ball" sounds like an early learning book for the under-fives.

There has been a progression in proper footballers' names over the years. It started with Wilf, Stan and Alf. Then came

Lucien, Bobby and Jimmy. They were followed by Roy, Ron, Don and Ray. Then there was Kevin, Trevor and Phil. The Terry, Tony, Gary era appeared (there were *two* Gary Stevens' in England's 1986 World Cup squad). And now we're into an era of Jermaines, Sols, Waynes and Rios. A good name does give you a start. I'm not saying it should be the first thing you think about as a prospective parent, but surely it's worth a moment's consideration: how easy will it be for little Algernon's/Terry's/Herbert's future team-mates to abbreviate him into a convincing football shout? He may thank you for it one day.

Up ahead of me Bob is moving around, thoughtfully laying the ball off to Simon. Simon is our centre forward. He went to school with me and Dan. He's tall and shaven-headed. He speaks in a low whisper. In the right light Simon looks like a football hooligan. In fact, he's a graphic designer and part-time DJ (birthdays and pub jukeboxes, but mainly his bedroom). He speaks in a whisper because he's very shy, in the way tall people sometimes are. In Sunday football, however, appearances are often enough. Every team needs someone who looks a bit like Simon.

Marshalled at the back by Keith – already furiously red-faced, nine minutes into the game – and with Lucien looking purposeful on the left, we're hustling the ball towards the outskirts of the blue-shirted defence. Our passing feels neat and rehearsed. Ten minutes in and we're not doing too badly.

It doesn't last. With a sense of inevitability, Dave horribly misjudges the bounce of the ball and suddenly two blue shirts are haring in on goal. Where's Keith? With a series of jerky movements that I know painfully well, he's sprinting across to cover. There's no need. The blue-shirted number ten rolls a delicately angled shot past Lars, spread on the edge of his area, arms waving at his sides like a man chasing chickens. The ball nuzzles gently into the corner of the net.

Lars seems to be rubbing both his shoulder and his calf muscle as he picks himself up. Hands on hips, Charlie punts the ball back downfield. Above us the sun has appeared as a gleaming white disc in the sky.

"We CAN'T give the FUCKING BALL away like that!"

"Sorry, lads. My fault," Dave says quietly.

"That is just too fucking SOFT!"

Shamefaced, we troop back towards the centre circle. Even Keith looks briefly downcast.

"Come on, whites. Watch that second ball," I say, feeling like a man talking to cover an awkward silence. Jerome claps me on the shoulder as he walks past.

"Way to go, girlfriend."

As Bob and Simon kick us off again the balance of the game has tilted. The blue shirts are moving quickly now. A tall, silver-booted midfielder seems to be controlling things from the centre circle. They're having fun, passing the ball around while we toil and track back. There's something depressing about watching another team enjoy themselves. It's like being a waiter at someone else's party.

"ONE OF YOU, FOR FUCK'S SAKE," Charlie shouts as Lucien and Simon both go to close down the silver-booted midfielder. Dan grits his teeth as he turns to chase.

"KEEP THE SHAPE! NO!"

"I'm covering that space."

"Hold your position."

"You're letting him go free."

"Stay on your man. He's mine."

"No he's not. He's not anyone's."

Sometimes it feels as though Charlie and Dan have been having the same argument for the last five years. It's like listening to a married couple bickering over where to go for Christmas. Not that it really seems to matter. By half-time we're 3–0 down and all notions of playing a season-igniting blinder have evaporated.

Despite this we're cheerful as we gather in the centre circle to drain our plates of orange quarters. Someone makes a joke about tiring the opposition out. Bob produces a flask of tea from somewhere.

"Not had your breakfast yet, Bob?"

"This is elevenses."

"Let us know if you fancy an early lunch."

"Did you see that centre half? Looks like my dad's pit-bull."

"Sssh, he'll hear you. They have a very acute sense of hearing."

Oh yes, we're pretty good at being 3–0 down at half-time. The morning haze has begun to clear and there's a watery sun that turns the grass a deep muddy green. Jerome and Dan are sitting sharing a bottle of water. Dave is leaning on Nev's shoulder as he reaches down to fiddle with a boot. Lars is looking pained as he explains something about his elbow to Lucien. Eventually Keith rouses himself to give his team talk.

"Lads, let's just keep our shape second half. No subs today so keep going the best you can. If you get injured, tough. No one's going to notice anyway."

The opposition are already lined up in formation and the referee has to call us back out. For the first few minutes of the half we keep the ball easily, knocking it around between us with the ease of a team that's been together for five long seasons. In a patch of sunlight Jerome beats two players and then beats them again, scampering in a tight circle that eventually takes him right back where he started.

"Jerome. Inside. Easy ball."

"Jerome, man on."

"Jerome, stop fucking about."

Skinny-legged, cuffs pulled over his wrists, he's finally dispossessed. Before long the blue shirts have scored again. This time it's a shot from the edge of the area that deflects with a deep thud off Nev's back and bobbles past a wrong-footed Lars in goal. He dives late and dramatically, but the ball is already spinning around in the orange netting.

We kick off again and Lucien sets off on one of his slaloming sprints from the left-hand touchline. A minor spat has begun to brew in the opposition defence. Despite being 4–0 up, they still don't seem very happy.

"For fuck's sake, blues, one of you."

"We should be dealing with that."

"Wanker."

The referee stops the game and calls their captain towards him. Dan is laughing about something with Charlie as the blue shirts sulkily take up their positions.

"Come on, girls, let's play nicely," Jerome says, but not too loudly, and Keith laughs horribly behind me. As we start again I have my best moment of the game, stepping away from two blue shirts and playing the ball backwards with the inside of my heel into the path of Dan. Even as it happens I know that this is the memory I'll keep from today. For a second the rest of the morning, the whole weekend, is just a backdrop; then it's gone and the game is accelerating towards the end.

With seconds left we score the final goal of the day. Lucien cuts inside and hits a powerful shot that chimes against a post before rebounding into the opposite corner. When the referee blows his whistle for full time it almost feels as though we've won.

A huge grey band of cloud is creeping across from behind the trees above the railway line, cutting the sky in half as we take the nets down. The ground has been churned into a drying cement of boot marks and divots. I kick a large clump in the direction of Dan as we walk back towards the changing rooms and he catches it in front of his chest.

Inside the air is damp with the smell of grass and heat from the showers. Nev's naked rump appears briefly as he shimmers into the thick steam at the back of the hut. Discarded items of kit accumulate in a pile in the middle of the tiled floor. Beneath the mud and sand there's a long, shallow cut on my thigh and a large purple bruise has appeared just below my knee.

Any Chance of a Game?

"Well played, lads. Fucking brilliant," Keith shouts, shirt-less and with his socks rolled down, clapping his hands as the last few bodies settle on the benches. There's some talk about Sunday afternoon drinks in the Bolingbroke down the road, but the truth is it's been a while since I've felt like going out for a beer after a game. Showered and changed I can already feel the powerful pull of home. Dan looks pale and glassy-eyed as he gathers his kit together.

There's always relief at the end, as well as tiredness. I'm already making my excuses, bag on my shoulder, as he joins me on the way out. I've got a bottle of water and a packet of Jaffa Cakes in the car. After that I can start to think about what that deep throbbing pain in my right knee might mean for the rest of the week. Another thing about playing football: after ninety minutes I will eat absolutely anything; and right now I'm starving.

2
First boots

Books about people who play football don't usually have much sense of scale. They tend just to concentrate on the bits you already know. The life story of a famous player will sprint at supersonic speed through being a kid, growing up and everything else that happens before fame and success. A typical opening chapter goes a bit like this:

AtschoolIonlyeverwantedtobeafootballermymumanddad wereagreatsupportIgotmyfirstbreakthenIsignedforUnited.

There we were before the big game. I turned to Robbo.

"This is the big one."

"Steveo," he said to me. "You're not wrong."

Then Big Macca walked in.

"Lads," he said. "This is it. The big one."

This, Robbo, Macca and me agreed, was definitely the big one.

After another three hundred pages Steveo's story usually finishes in one of two ways:

And so I retired from playing football
(a) grateful that I'd never again have to work with
such a collection of two-faced amateurs;
or
(b) delighted to be still very much part of the game
through my role as assistant hand-shaker in the magnif-
icent new Pot Noodle stand.

I'm a football journalist, so I spend a lot of time reading this kind of stuff. I write articles for football magazines or the football pages of newspapers. Now and then people ask how you get into doing a job like mine. I haven't really got an answer, beyond exhausting all the more sensible career options you might have; and then facing up to the one thing you always secretly wanted to do all along. It can be a bit up and down at times. I'm tempted to say something like "it's a living" or "it pays the bills", but it doesn't really. I'm not complaining though. My bank might be – and my mum occasionally – but not me.

I played my first proper game of football twenty years ago. Since then I've been in a team pretty much every year of my life. I grew up in south-east London, and between the ages of five and eleven I spent most of my time at Elmvale Primary School, a low yellow-brick building with a willow tree by the front gate.

Elmvale school was halfway up the hill from Deptford to Brockley. This suited it pretty well. At the top of the hill the streets widened out and there were trees and big, crumbling terraced houses with front gardens. By local standards at least,

Brockley was definitely a top-of-the-hill kind of place. And Elmvale was definitely a halfway-up-the-hill kind of school.

Not that I knew anything about this at the time. I was a shy kid, wispy and pale, but awkward too. My first school photo, the one that gets sent home in a gilt-edged cardboard frame, shows half a grin sandwiched between big collars, stick-out hair, gammy eyes and an expression which still, somehow, manages to suggest that if you don't stop muscling in on my used *Star Wars* figures racket I'll have some of my people take you for a long walk around the netball courts. Every primary school class has a skinny kid with hand-me-down clothes who specialises in throwing up and occasionally wetting himself in public. I wasn't quite that kid, but I certainly hung out with him – until he dropped me for the tiny boy with the big head who cries a lot.

Our school was very new at the time. A lot of the teachers were young. They had ideas about how things should be done. We may not have learned maths properly but we certainly got a solid grounding in the basic principles of doing modern dance in your underwear. We sang calypso songs and had disturbing sex education lessons, the high point of which involved one of our teachers bringing in her own placenta wrapped in kitchen foil. We lined up and took turns to touch it. Three of my classmates had to go home early.

To anybody who grew up then, the early 1980s were, on the face of it, a golden era for child mortality. We flew kites next to electricity pylons. We fell into canals or went swimming shortly after eating a meal. Without warning we ran out from behind ice-cream vans into oncoming Austin Allegros. And in the evenings we walked along railway tracks and returned to inspect lit fireworks.

At least this is what the constant stream of public information films we were shown at school would have you believe. But in truth, if Elmvale had a problem it was a distinct lack of danger about the place. Playing the soundtrack to *Watership Down* in assembly is all very well, but sometimes when you're eight years old you just need to rock out.

Fortunately there was a place you could go when you needed some excitement. The school playground was made up of a series of grey concrete terraces joined by flights of knee-grazingly sharp steps. There were spiky bushes and a little wooded area that nobody ever paid any attention to. Most importantly, at the top of all this, there was a large concrete rectangle enclosed on all sides by a high wire fence. Someone had painted purple psychedelic shapes on the ground. There were hopscotch patterns too and some faded cartoon animals. There was no disguising it, though. No school, however soft-pedalled, has ever managed to get rid of football.

Kids aren't fussy. Any piece of ground can be a playground. A set of low white metal goals had been left embedded in the concrete at either end, and this was all the encouragement we needed. Inside the cage life was a constant kickabout, which began as soon as a minimum of two had arrived and could swell to as many as thirty a side. It wasn't just football. It was here in the concrete cage that I first learned to show off and make inadequate small talk with girls. And it was here that I had my first proper fight with a boy called Mickey – which ended with me getting in one lame, open-handed slap and then running away to hide behind a crowd of very young girls. Which is still, incidentally, the best way to win a fight.

The football pitch had a profound effect on all of us. Suddenly there was something to do at school, something anybody could join in. I made friends. Or, at least, now there were some people who actually knew my name. After a while I just couldn't get enough. Every break time, before school, after school, I wanted to spend my whole life in between those two white goals.

If I'm honest, the summer holidays were often quite lonely; all that free time and suddenly nothing to fill it with. At the end of my first year of football the holidays stretched away endlessly into the distance, six weeks of afternoons in an empty park, the sound of distant ice-cream vans, and long evenings waiting for something to happen. I celebrated by spending two solid weeks kicking a ball against a wall in our garden. It was just like being at school, only without any of the lessons or any of the friends.

I lived with my mum and my brother Jack in a large, dusty house on a long and boring tree-lined road. My dad had gone to live in South America when I was two years old and he was still out there. He sent birthday cards and football shirts, which seemed all right, and even pretty exciting, at the time. Jack was three years older than me, an age gap that, by the time you're adults, you have to remind yourself isn't actually very big. He collected comics and fiddled with his bike. We used to spend hours in our bedroom, gradually smashing up our collection of toy cars, but it was always me outside kicking a ball against the kerb and wondering why all the houses looked so tall and empty.

Something important did happen that summer, however. My mum bought me my first pair of football boots. We went down together to the sports shop on Deptford High Street. The shop was a dark room with boxes piled up to the ceiling. It smelt of leather and fresh plastic. The moment I first set eyes on the boots, I knew I had to have them.

They were black and purple with a long tongue lolling out at the front. Compared to the squashy brown lace-ups and low-tech plimsolls I'd been raised on, they looked like a product of some alien intelligence from the distant future. Excitingly, they had a large silver 'P' on the side, after Patrick, the company that made them. It was from here that a potent, charismatic and occasionally confusing figure first entered my eight-year-old consciousness: Kevin Keegan.

I already knew who he was of course. In 1982 Kevin Keegan was huge: the most famous footballer in the world, England captain and the face of a thousand breakfast cereals. He was Mighty Mouse, Super Kev and Special K. He had teenage fans. He had his own brand of knitwear. He was also the face of Patrick boots, a small French sportswear company. Using the simple tactic of offering him a huge amount of money, Patrick had managed to tempt Keegan into wearing their boots. On the back of this, sales went through the roof. Patrick would keep Super Kev on the payroll after he retired, paying him to travel around the world flogging their gear. This seems to have been the kiss of death for the company. "Sadly, within twelve months they went bust," Kevin later revealed in his autobiography.

In the summer of 1982 something in me recognised Kevin Keegan, Mr Patrick boots, as my personal ambassador in the wider world. There he was on TV playing for England at the World Cup. It didn't work out for Kevin in Spain. He was at the point in his career where the level of his celebrity was starting to overtake his actual powers. He missed an easy header that would have put England through to the quarter-finals. I can still remember him holding his head in his hands as the ball went wide. Even as an eight-year-old I couldn't help wondering if the problem wasn't something to do with his hairstyle.

As the school year came rolling around again, I wore my Patrick boots in my first proper game, for Elmvale under-nines against local rivals Hardstaff Gardens. The game took place on a sunny afternoon in early autumn, and it was a massacre. It was always going to be a massacre. There was history there. Hardstaff were tougher than us. We knew it, and so did they.

Hardstaff weren't just from the bottom of the hill. They *were* the bottom of the hill. When you went out of our front gates and looked left it was the first thing you saw, a slab of grey concrete crouched behind high borstal railings. The kids were harder too. This applied across the board. My brother went there and, despite being something close to the school swot, he was still surprisingly tough. He never made the football team, but this wasn't surprising given that he failed to meet the basic selection criteria of thighs like a World's Strongest Man contestant and a full-face beard by the age of ten.

We were driven to the game in our school minibus. Even in the excitement of it all, there was still a sense of some vague doom awaiting us, like prisoners being taken down to the cells. Every playground has a leader. We had Eric. He was small and serious-looking, but somehow everybody knew right from the start that he was in charge.

"We're the A-Team. You can be Hannibal. I'm Face," he told me as we pulled out of the school gates.

"I want to be Face," someone objected.

"Bagsie Hannibal. Hannibal smokes."

"Wait a second," Eric started again. "*I'm* Face ..."

"I'm BA."

"No way."

"Yes way."

"No though."

"Yes though."

"Forget about it. We're not the A-Team. We're someone else," Eric sighed.

There was a pause. "We're *Star Wars*," a voice suggested.

"Bagsie Luke."

"Shut up. Shut up. Shut up. You're idiots."

"Bagsie Han."

"Bagsie the Emperor."

Actually we could have done with the Emperor on our side. Certainly, it didn't feel as though the force was exactly with us. The game was played on a men's pitch with proper full-sized goals. It took four of us to carry one of the square wooden posts to the hole in the ground where it could be wobbled upright. Until then my school friends and I had been the absolute limits of each other's playtime footballing world. Now, suddenly, we were team-mates wearing a strange red and white kit and walking the plank together out on to a huge municipal pitch. From first whistle to last we were torn to pieces.

Hardstaff attacked us head-on. The long punt downfield was followed by five or six galloping forwards, big kids with sharp knees and long legs and proper muscles. We lost 5–0. It should have been more but the pitch, thank God, really was very big. It was a savage introduction. Back then it was still a shock to realise that you could have all your friends around you, have your Patrick boots on your feet, and still lose so wretchedly.

I'd been reading *Roy of the Rovers* comics. The stories had always seemed completely believable. During a match Roy had time for lengthy and often very pedantic conversations. In the moment it took Roy's Rocket, his powerful shot, to leave his boot and hit the top corner of the net there was opportunity for people in the crowd to exchange portentous remarks ("Racey's going to have a crack. This should test the keeper with neither team happy for a draw." "Yes.").

In real life football was mayhem. We spent the first ten minutes in a state of total confusion, like swimmers desperately trying to keep our heads above the water. Hardstaff were relentless. How could they possibly be enjoying this? Early in the first half Eric picked up the ball and started scuttling towards the halfway line, only to be set upon by four or five green shirts and left capsized in the mud.

At least by the end something interesting had begun to happen. At 5–0 down we started to behave like a football team. We kept the ball for a while. We had a shot at goal. Our goalkeeper, Sam, in a huge yellow jersey, was shouting and shaking his head, in the style of all goalkeepers everywhere since the beginning of recorded time. And at some point it clicked. This was what it was like to be in a team, out in the middle of all that grass, with just an opposition and a ball dragging you from one side to the other.

All I can really remember of my own performance is one enormous clearance near the touchline that had to be retrieved from the fourth pitch along. Everybody approved of this. And to this day, long punted clearances that go miles out of play are still the surest way I've found of earning your team-mates' respect.

On the way back we sat together feeling like survivors of some terrible battle. It's tempting to measure every team you ever play in against your first. Either way Elmvale has always stuck with me. We walked out on to the pitch together, we lost together and we pretended we weren't really that bothered on the bus home together.

"We're like *Star Trek*," someone suggested.

"Shut up," Eric said.

"I'm Captain Kirk."

"Shut up."

"You're Spock."

"I'm never Spock."

"Captain Kirk's a girl."

"Spock's a girl."

"Don't cuss Spock. Spock's well hard. Spock's got the death grip."

There are some things you do for the first time and think, yes, this is me. Forget all the other stuff. This is what I'm supposed to be doing. Things like driving a car, having sex, or getting drunk – although preferably not all at the same time. For me, playing football was the first time I ever got that feeling. We may have lost heavily, and it may have been, at times, a deeply confusing experience; but something definitely changed that day.

Once you get the football rhythm into your system it stays with you. Even now it takes control of my week. Usually I'm the sort of person who runs up a flight of stairs. Put me on an escalator and I can't stand still. Come to think of it, I can be a real pain in the arse. I know this because, for a couple of days after a game, I'm a different kind of person. Suddenly it's me taking the steps down to the Tube one at a time and holding on to the handrail for dear life. This is what playing football on a Sunday can do to you; particularly when you're nearly thirty years old and the only exercise you get is playing football on a Sunday.

There are ways of avoiding it. After a game I should probably warm down and stretch for half an hour. I should rehydrate. Instead of doing that I have a drink of chalky water from the tap on the wall outside the changing rooms, then I sit hunched in a car for half an hour, and finally I put my feet up on the sofa and pretend to be awake for the rest of the afternoon. Laura used to find it funny that I could get in such a state. These days I try to keep it to myself.

By Wednesday, though, everything's almost back to normal. My usual way of walking has returned. I can sit down in a chair without sighing deeply. And memories of Sunday have completed that strange process of transforming themselves into something else, reconstructed as pleasure rather than pain.

Come Thursday morning I'm ready to go again. It's almost the weekend, time for a long lunch, a slow Saturday afternoon and thoughts about early morning starts. Keith sends around his email telling us who and where and when, and exactly what's going to happen to us if we don't turn up. And everything builds towards Sunday and that feeling of being out in open country between two white goals with wet feet, familiar voices and a feeling that, for a couple of hours at least, anything might happen.

3
Back to school

Sunday October 11th 2004
King George IV vs. Bolingbroke Athletic

I used to share a flat with Dan. We lived together on the top
floor of a large house wedged in between a builder's yard and
the back of a supermarket. Despite our occasional attempts at
housework the place was always dirty. The windows were
caked with grit and there was a constant fur of dust on the
carpets and on the stairs. For some reason the kitchen floor had
been laid with white plastic tiles, which showed up every smear
of grime like a map of the Greek Islands. It used to bother me
until I decided to stop wearing my glasses while I was at home.
After a few months we didn't bother turning on the overhead
lights any more, which also helped.

At times things did drift a little. Once, after a long night in
the pub across the road, which had a late licence and a club in
the back room, I threw up in the downstairs bathroom.
Unfortunately the toilet already contained a screwed-up take-
away bag. There were chips floating in the bowl and an
uneaten chicken drumstick poking above the water line.
Tackling the problem head-on, I gathered up the whole
mixture in a plastic bin bag, cutting my hand on a broken wine
glass in the process, bundled the bag downstairs, and stuffed it

into a dustbin just as the front door closed behind me. Fortunately it was a sunny day. Decorated with sick and fast food, smeared with blood from the cut on my hand, and still in my underwear, I was discovered asleep on the front steps an hour later by our downstairs neighbour.

It wasn't all bad. We had a mini beer fridge by the television and plastic pellet guns that you could fire across the living room. There was a huge sofa, from which you could look through the big picture window at the peeling terrace on the other side of the road, and an open house policy for anyone who wanted to drop by.

The flat is still there in a narrow grid of quiet streets just south of the River Thames. The rooms are big and the place actually scrubs up quite well once you've cleared it up a bit. I used to like living there. I say used to, but actually I'm still really in the process of moving out. Half of my stuff is lying around the place. The answer machine is mine. So is the toaster and the chair in the living room.

"Have we got any milk? This is finished."

"You might."

"Might what?"

"Have some milk. At your house. I haven't got any."

I'm having breakfast with Dan in the kitchen. The blinds are drawn, keeping out the Sunday morning sun. He's drinking a can of Coke and cutting a thick slice off a piece of Cheddar wrapped in paper. We're playing in Dulwich today. It was easy enough to stop round on the way. My football gear is still here anyway.

"Go on, get me some milk. I'm your guest."

"I told you. I haven't got any."

"This place is already falling apart."

He cuts another chunk of cheese and eats it slowly.

"It's good actually, having it to myself. I could get used to it."

The kitchen hasn't changed much. There are newspapers and CD cases piled up on the table and an overflowing ashtray balanced on the oven hob. Around the bin the build-up of rubbish has given way to a policy of piling bottles and cans in its general location. The contents of the fridge look just the same as they always did. In fact, they probably are the same. It's a strange mixture in there: left-over pizza boxes, fillet steak, a half-eaten Scotch egg in the butter dish and three bottles of champagne on the top shelf.

Dan may live a little bit like a caveman, but he actually earns quite a lot of money at his bank in the City. As I said, I don't know what he does exactly, but it seems to have absolutely no bearing on what he gets up to outside of office hours. When he got his bonus last year we celebrated, not with a weekend in New York, but with a twelve-hour bender in New Cross. The night ended with us being chased across a building site by a group of kids who had spent the last two hours trying to sell us a foil package full of what looked like household detergent.

"I don't come round to your house and look in the fridge," Dan says, finishing the cheese and lighting a cigarette.

"You don't come round at all."

"That's because I haven't been invited."

"Since when do you need to be?"

"Since you moved into your girlfriend's house and stopped hanging out with your mates."

He coughs thoughtfully, swinging his feet off the back of the chair in front of him.

"What does it take to get you to actually leave this flat?"

"An invitation."

"All right. I invite you to get off your arse and come over to my place once in a while."

He grins as he stands up and zips his jacket. "You mean our place."

We stop to pick up Jerome and Simon in Tooting, and join the gentle drift of Sunday morning traffic towards Dulwich. It's one of those late autumn mornings where the sky is a cold hard blue and the sun never seems to rise above the level of the trees. Jerome is wearing a baseball cap under his hood. Next to him Simon is folded uncomfortably across the back seat, apologetically tall.

"It was Keith's birthday last night."

"Oh shit. Did anyone go?"

"Uh-uh. I thought you lot might have. You live near him."

"I do. He doesn't."

"Simon?"

Simon shakes his head. Keith invited us all along last Sunday. He even sent me a text message during the week.

"I saw him in the Rose and Crown," Dan yawns. "With his mates. It took me quite a long time to get away from him."

"I wonder what kind of state he's in this morning."

"A bad one judging by last night. He wouldn't stop talking about his shoes."

"His what?"

"New shoes. Brown. Horrible. He made me look at them. He said he was going out on the pull in his new shoes."

"Good to see he's all grown up now."

"Oi, Mr B, can you slow down? We're getting mashed up in the back."

I've started to weave through a dog-leg of backstreets around the South Circular. It's something I do automatically around here, I know it so well. That's the thing about today's game. We're playing at our old school. We all went here, Dan and Simon and me, from the age of eleven through to eighteen. This happens once a season: George IV use a pitch out on the eastern end of our old playing fields.

The main building looks just the same as it always did. Even the trees and the cars in the car park look the same. It's strange that it should be football that brings us back, because it was never really a football school. Rugby and hockey were the main winter activities. Football was a minority sport played by a few diehards. It was also how I first got to know Dan.

Rugby is a game for hooligans played by gentlemen; football is a game for gentlemen played by hooligans. That was what they taught us at school – literally in fact: it was one of the examples of a good sentence in our English grammar. The football pitches were stuck away in a far corner of the playing fields. Our coach was Mr Gomersall, also known as Gonad.

Gonad was from Yorkshire. He taught geography but he'd played football to a decent level and he was known as a hard case. If you stepped out of line during swimming lessons he used to make you lie down in the freezing cold, verucca-ridden footbath at the entrance to the pool.

He wasn't quite as bad during football, although this didn't stop him from treating the game as though it was an offshoot of rugby league or tag-team wrestling. "Boys, you've got to go in hard from the start," he told us aged twelve. "Physical presence. The first time you come up against your man go straight through him. He won't forget it."

So today's pitch is a familiar one. Even the ancient square wooden goalposts look the same. It's rare in a city like London to find something that ties you to a place over so many years. But here we are, back again with our shorts and boots and looking for a game.

We may be here, but Keith isn't. This is a problem because, besides being our inspirational skipper, he's also got the kit bag.

"It's those drinks. I bet he's still in bed."

"I've been calling him," Charlie says. "No answer."

We're sitting on a low wall outside the changing rooms. The sun is slightly higher in the sky but we're all still wearing coats and scarves.

"He'll be here soon. There's plenty of time." Bob is wearing a woolly hat and gold half-rim spectacles. He's reading the *Observer*. It has to be said, he doesn't really look like a footballer. Dan and Jerome are sharing a Walkman, a single earpiece each. Nev is bundled up in an enormous Puffa jacket that makes him look like a snowman.

The George are already changed and out on the pitch warming up. Their ginger-haired skipper has been across a few times to ask when we're going to be ready. By now we've decided to ignore him.

"We should be keeping warm. Come on, let's do some stretches."

"Charlie, give it a rest."

"League rules say if we're more than an hour late it's a walkover."

"Are you kidding? This isn't the Premiership. Anyway it's Keith. He'll turn up."

"Maybe he went out in his new shoes and pulled. Maybe he's blown us out."

"No chance," Dan says firmly. "Keith never pulls."

"Hold on. What's this?"

A smudged white estate car judders into view on the main road and makes a right turn towards us. A familiar head and thick neck loom in outline in the passenger seat. Keith leaps out and heaves the kit bag on to his shoulder, nearly bending double under its weight.

"What does he look like?"

"All right, lads."

Unshaven and still greasy with booze, Keith staggers across and drops the bag on the ground. Behind him, a wiry figure in a baseball cap and bomber jacket follows him out of the car. This is the Hawk, Keith's best mate. Keith's friends are a strange bunch. The Hawk has played for us now and then. The last time, I came off the pitch with a headache from the two of them shouting at each other.

"Minicab," Keith says. "Someone get it will you? I feel like absolute shite and I've got to get in there right now, so don't ask me any questions."

He disappears inside the changing rooms just as the George's ginger-haired captain hovers into view again.

"All present and correct. If you'll just give us a moment to take instructions from our captain," Bob says, as the sounds of Keith being sick emerge from the nearest window.

"You're lucky we're here at all. He was way too wasted to drive," the Hawk says as we troop inside and a white-faced Keith appears in the doorway to the dressing room.

"Right, lads, what are we waiting for? Let's get out there."

Lining up for kick-off I notice he's started shaking as he ties up his boots. It seems to have spread through the rest of us too. Jerome only removes his coat as the referee blows his whistle. And right from the start everything seems to be moving in slow motion.

"Come on, Boligs," the Hawk shouts from a horizontal position on the halfway line, as Nev punts a long pass towards Simon in attack. The ball holds up on the wind and bounces at least twenty yards out of play. The minicab driver has stayed to watch. He shakes his head as I go across to chase a wayward pass near the touchline.

"In hard, George. We should be beating these," the ginger-haired skipper says as another passing move peters out on the far side.

"Pick this up, whites," Charlie shouts back and for once I'm grateful for the sound of his voice, for any sign of urgency. Dan seems to be running around gamely in midfield, but the rest of us are moving at half-speed. Fortunately the George aren't much better. They score just once in the first half and it's a freak goal, a corner kick from the left that hangs on the wind and then bends in wickedly at the near post.

"Never seen that before," someone says as we wander back for the restart.

Shortly afterwards, as a green-shirted George player goes to take a throw-in, a large brown dog appears on the pitch in a forward position.

"Put that thing on a fucking lead," the Hawk shouts from the other side of the pitch. Even the minicab driver looks outraged as a barrage of abuse is directed towards the dog's owner, a middle-aged man out for a Sunday morning walk. He collars the dog and retreats to a safe distance as the throw is cleared violently by Keith into the trees on the near side.

I'm always wary of people on the touchline. It must go back to the parents who used to watch when we were kids playing in the South London junior leagues. Every other game would throw up a psycho dad. Usually the psycho dad takes a while to warm up. You can spot him if you look closely: hands in pockets, shaking his head and paying just a little bit too much attention to the game. He announces himself by suddenly shouting, "FOR FUCK'S SAKE, WHAT THE FUCK WAS THAT, SON?" as two skinny ten-year-olds challenge for the ball. By the end of the first half a genuine psycho dad will be bouncing on his heels, haranguing the coach and anybody else within earshot, and standing in an even bigger empty space on the touchline than he started in.

The real problems started when we had more than one psycho dad around at any given time. Conflict was never far away.

"Come on now, Darren. *We're* not going to resort to that kind of thing."

"Kevin, son, we're better than this."

"Don't complain about it, boy. Just get in there and give him some back."

Once I saw two psycho dads actually rolling about on the ground, having decided to "sort" things in the car park after the game. Other families stepped around them on the way back to their cars, pretending nothing was happening.

Half-time comes as a relief. It feels as though we've been asleep for the last forty-five minutes. This is football with a hangover. We gather on the clubhouse steps. We've got a good view of the school from here, but I don't feel any real connection to it. Coming back here these last five seasons with Keith and Jerome and everyone else, playing on the same patch of grass, has taken away the strangeness. I've got other things to worry about at the moment. Such as the realisation, as we settle down with bottles of water in the sun and Bob starts reading the newspaper again, that this is probably the worst I've ever seen us play.

"How old are you anyway?" Jerome asks, standing over Keith's prostrate body. He seems to be sweating very heavily for someone who has barely moved for the last half-hour.

"Thirty."

"Is that why you're in this state? Going out proving you've still got it."

"Yeah, that's right."

"Oh my God. What's that on your face?"

Beneath his deep-set eyes and above the horrible expanse of his beard, Keith has a smudge of yellow swelling.

"Got clobbered by someone last night."

"When they threw you out," the Hawk says from under his baseball cap.

"Yeah, well. Enough said about that."

Keith's not the only one of us turning thirty soon. I'm twenty-nine. Dan's twenty-eight. And Bob must be at least fifty. The rest of the Bolingbroke squad are either late twenties or mid-thirties, with the exception of Jerome and Charlie. Over the last season or so we've played a few teams where almost all of their players are younger than us. There are still plenty of exceptions: mid-life crisis left-wingers, ancient goalkeepers, and huge cardiac-ripe centre halves. But they're getting fewer. And the youngest ones really are starting to look young.

"Ask him what happened when he got chucked out," the Hawk leers as we get up to go back out for the second half, his breath thick with something semi-digested. "Ask him about his shoes."

With the end of the game in sight we start to pick things up a bit. Charlie manages to coax us into a decent ten minutes or so of chasing and harrying. Keith has found an unexpected rush of energy from somewhere and Dan is getting the best of things in midfield. Pushing forward on the left side Lucien finds himself in space and curls a diagonal pass right across the face of the George goal as the green shirts scatter and someone completely misses their kick.

Jerome meets the cross first time and sends the ball flashing back into the far corner of the net before the goalkeeper can move. He's off and running straight away, pulling his shirt up over his head, arms spread as he heads back towards the halfway line.

"That one's for you, Keith," he shouts, dodging sideways away from Nev. "Keith's birthday goal!"

"It was yesterday."

"Come on, whites. Let's go again. We can win this."

Unbelievably, we're level. But this is as good as it gets. With ten minutes left Bob miscues a volley that smacks full into the face of a green-shirted defender. He collapses sideways on to the turf and something terrible happens. We get the giggles. This has never happened before. It takes us all by surprise. As the George player gets to his feet I'm still trying to stop myself cracking up. Putting his fist in his mouth, Keith looks like he's about to die. It's like being back at school. Which is, I suppose, exactly where I am.

With the exception of Charlie, short-legged and persistent in midfield, nobody's really concentrating on the game any more. With a few minutes left the green shirts find themselves through on goal, three of them in space where Keith might have been if he hadn't been getting his breath back near the corner flag. A toe-poked shot is well saved by Lars. The rebound falls to another green shirt who blasts the ball into the empty net and turns away with a loud shout that surprises me.

As we walk off at the end of a 2–1 defeat Charlie and Dan are both shaking their heads before they've even reached the touchline.

"All right?" I say, catching up with Dan.

"Fine."

"You don't look it."

Up ahead of us Keith has thrown his arm around Nev's shoulder and is being helped from the field.

"That was a waste of time. We were rubbish," he says.

"Yeah. Well, you know. It's just a game."

"Not really fair on the other side, though, is it?"

"Since when did that matter? Anyway, they only just beat us."

We stop outside the changing rooms as Jerome and Dave go straight inside. I don't really know what we're waiting for. A very loud aeroplane is passing overhead, making us shout above the roar.

"It's all right for you, though," Dan says. "You don't really give a shit any more."

"What?"

"It's not just you. Look at Keith. We're a shambles all round these days."

It's not like Dan to be bothered like this. He's wrong, though. I do give a shit. Just not perhaps quite as much of a shit as I used to. You can't keep on giving a shit about everything in equal amounts. Not for ever, not when life only gets more, and not less, complicated as time goes by. In the end you've only got a finite amount of shit to give.

It's unusually noisy inside. The Hawk and Keith are yelling at each other across the room and Bob is singing in a deep voice in the showers. Red-faced and basted with sweat, Nev is deep in conversation with Jerome and Lucien.

"Lads," Keith says, spotting us in the doorway. "Straight back down the boozer this afternoon. I'll come in the car with you, Dave can take the rest in the Volvo."

And so half an hour later, partly to prove that I still give a shit, I'm at the bar in the Spanish Galleon Tavern, buying drinks while the Hawk and Keith keep up their shouted conversation at our table in the corner. Bob, Nev, Jerome and Simon have turned out too. Dan is communing with the fruit machine on his own. After my third pint of lager the tiredness starts to lift and turn into something else. I can feel the afternoon begin to fade away and all I want to do is stay here and keep drinking and forget about everything outside this dim, brown-carpeted room.

"Barbecue is the weirdest crisp flavour," Keith is saying.

"Why?"

"It's not a real flavour. It's not even a proper food. Not like salt and vinegar or cheese and onion. A barbecue is just a way of cooking things. It's like having toaster flavour crisps or saucepan flavour."

"Prawn cocktail. Smoky bacon. He's right. All the others are proper foods."

"I think it's meant to be barbecue sauce flavour."

"Even if it is, so what? What kind of barbecue sauce? You can barbecue anything."

"You can barbecue a cauliflower."

"Exactly. You can light a barbecue and not put anything on it at all."

"Keith. You really do talk a lot of shit."

Dan sits down at the end of the table and reaches across to take the Hawk's lighter.

"What happened to your shoes last night?"

"What shoes?"

"The new ones. You told me you were going out to pull in your new shoes."

The Hawk starts laughing and Keith looks unexpectedly sheepish.

"Stolen, mate. Gone. Don't fucking ask."

He gets up and staggers off towards the gloomy recess at the back of the bar. The Hawk watches him go.

"Last night," he says. "We ended up in this club. Keith could hardly stand up. He got himself in a spot of bother on the dance floor. The bouncers came over and carried him out, three of them. In the crush someone runs up and rips off his shoes. Nicked them. Keith had to walk home in his socks."

There's a silence around the table.

"Just like that?"

"He was gutted."

"I bet. We'll just have to make sure we don't mention it too often."

Eventually it's time to leave. The silent alarm inside my

head, telling me I should have been home four hours ago, has become too insistent to ignore. I steel myself to get up, eat a handful of peanuts for the journey and gather my bags. Dan won't be coming with me. He's at the bar, chatting up a couple of girls who can't be much more than sixteen. He gives me a quizzical look as I stand up.

"Going home?"

"Yeah. Don't start."

"I'm not. Maybe see you in the week. I was only messing about earlier."

"I'll email you."

"Say hi to Laura from me."

"I will."

"Tell her I'm still here if she changes her mind."

By the time I get home it's dark. The evening has already begun to fade into the first thoughts of Monday and the week to come. The lights are on in the hall, as they were when I left this morning, and there's a smell of cooking coming from the kitchen.

"That was a long day," Laura says from the top of the stairs as I take off my coat.

"It was Keith's birthday. We went for drinks."

My legs have seized up on the way home and it takes a while to climb the stairs. Laura has been out all afternoon. There are shopping bags in the hall and the signs of dinner hastily prepared, and I'm aware that yet again the weekend has been sliced in two by football, disappearing in a familiar routine before I've had the chance to do half the things I might have wanted.

"Did you win?" she asks.

"Not really."

Outside the streetlamps are already glowing orange and a pale moon has appeared as I open the back door to dump the bag with my boots outside in the small, quietly mouldering garden shed. I've tried to find somewhere else to put them, but this is the only place that's already sufficiently unpleasant. Inside the shed it smells of grass and damp cardboard and leather. In fact, it smells just like football.

4
Girls

Gigantic DIY superstores are God's way of telling you some-thing. What they're telling you is: you don't like gigantic DIY superstores. Without them we just couldn't be sure.

It's Sunday afternoon and I'm at Homebase in Acton with Laura. Nobody likes doing this kind of thing. As you walk in through the automatic door your trolley veers off course, goug-ing your shin with its rear fender. A maze of plastic furniture funnels you down pathways lined with swing-seats and terra-cotta pots. Green-aproned staff wander past, men with pencils behind their ears study kitchen fittings, and somewhere in a corridor nearby a baby is crying very loudly.

"Can you reach that? It's a bit high for me. No, the one above."

"Just ... a second."

"What are you doing?"

"Resting."

"Never mind. Here's a man. Thanks."

Laura leaves me in the bedroom section while she heads off outside, disappearing down the long central aisle towards the palm fronds and statuettes. Bedroom isn't such a bad place to be.

It's almost like being at home, almost like being in your bedroom. Except, in common with many people, I've never owned a quilted floral bedspread or a huge white plastic headboard.

It has been a difficult weekend. This morning, on a drying pitch, we were overwhelmed by a bunch of thirtysomething skinheads teamed up with a pair of fresh-faced teenage forwards. Faced with this blend of youth and experience we defended for seventy minutes before slipping beneath the waves like a sinking trawler. I did a lot of chasing, lunging and falling over.

Through a side door in Bedroom there's an entire mocked-up bedroom suite, complete with table, curtains and stuffed toy tiger. Only the ceiling breaks the spell, the four walls joined by a distant corrugated plastic roof, through which there are traces of dull afternoon rain. The bed is soft and cool. I lie down and close my eyes for a moment. "I'm sorry. It's okay. He's with me," a voice is saying, suddenly, as a green apron disappears out of the bedroom door. The grey-backed window with its drawn curtains looks familiar. But something isn't quite… Standing over me, Laura has a small tray of herbs under her arm and a pot plant in a clear plastic bag.

"Sorry. I dozed off."

"This is hopeless," she says. "You lot on a Sunday, it's like looking after chimpanzees."

"Chimpanzees?"

"Not even grown-up ones. Baby chimpanzees. You jump up and down together. You do a lot of shouting. Then you get tired and have to lie down."

"So basically what you're saying is we're lots of fun to be around."

"Not exactly. But close."

"I feel your anger."

"No you don't."

Laura doesn't like football. The game just doesn't do anything for her. When it's on television all she sees is confusion, a foreign culture, an hour and a half of sweaty indignation. Given a choice between football and reruns of *Will & Grace*, football and an afternoon reading a book and football and a brisk walk in the park, there's only ever one winner. Fortunately it doesn't play a particularly big part in her life. Most of the time, like millions of other people, she can quite happily ignore it. In fact, the only reason Laura knows for sure that she doesn't like football is that she lives with me.

Before we met she'd never even watched a match. This still seems incredible. It was like stumbling across a lost tribe in the Amazon who've never seen a car or drunk Coca-Cola. It didn't last long. These days Laura has seen a huge amount of football – without, it has to be said, ever showing any signs of interest. When Michael Owen scored for England against Portugal at Euro 2004 she jumped around the living room with me before she realised anything unusual had happened. God knows what she thought I was doing.

It's a shame Laura doesn't like football. She could be quite handy. She's tall and slim and she's got a good engine. You should see her run for a bus. But I have to admit it can be a real eye-opener living with somebody who doesn't like football. It gives you a whole new way of looking at things. As you put down your muddy bag, open the Goals! pullout in your Sunday newspaper and settle in for an afternoon of Sky Sports, it can really make you think. Mainly it makes me think, why doesn't she like football?

A lot of people are interested in the game now who wouldn't have been before. It's hard to say exactly when football started to become fashionable. Some would point to the effects of the 1990 World Cup in Italy, the start of the Premiership a couple of years later and the game's shift into the world of celebrity and popular culture over the decade that followed.

For me, the moment I realised football had changed for ever came a few years later. During the mid-Nineties there was an advert on TV for Bodyform sanitary towels. In the usual style, it featured a woman roller skating in a white Lycra catsuit, as well as a football match. Just before the start of the "whooo-aaaah! Body-fo-orm!" jingle, the camera cut to two teams of women playing in the shadow of a mountain range. A useful-looking attack was mounted down the wing. The ball was crossed into the centre, where a girl with dreadlocks rose impressively and powered a header into the net.

Not many people appreciate this, but the Bodyform goal was an almost perfect reconstruction of Ruud Gullit's opener for Holland in the 1988 Euro Championship Final. In that game the ball was swung in from the left, Gullit leapt high and, dreadlocks flapping, nodded it past the Russian keeper. Football had truly entered the biological heart of the mainstream.

Laura isn't the kind of girl who'll pretend to be interested in something. You won't catch her wearing her boyfriend's replica shirt on a night in or making remarks about pies. Which is all absolutely fine by me. There's more than enough football in every other part of my week. Actually, Laura is being nice to me today. We've had a very long weekend. And yesterday was basically a nightmare. We went to a wedding. Even worse than that, it was the wedding of two close friends.

Life is very different when you live with a woman. It smells much better for a start. The bathroom is clean. The fridge has stuff like yoghurt and cottage cheese in it. And there are some things you just can't rush. Getting ready to go out is one of them. Getting ready to go out to a wedding, on the other hand, takes you to another level completely.

I find it pretty easy to decide what to wear on days like these, mainly because there's no real decision to make. I've got one good suit, one shirt without holes or smudges and one tie that I like. It takes about five minute to put it all on and another five to find my smart shoes. The shoes aren't actually that smart any more. They've got to the stage where you can pretty much see the exact shape of my feet in the creases of the leather. I can't bring myself to buy new ones though, mainly because they're actually a very good pair from when I used to have a proper job.

While Laura went through the various stages of gearing herself up for a public appearance, I had time to hit the shops, go to the bookies next to the off-licence with the iron bars on the window, and call Dan to work out the best way of him getting over here to pick us up for the drive.

"I think head west and then north."

"West is no go. Semi-permanent traffic calming works. Lane blockage and temporary roundabout."

"Try the Embankment."

"Gridlock over the river. Sheer weight of traffic plus two sets of lights out."

"Well, I don't know then."

"It's your manor. What's the back route?"

"I've only been here three weeks. I still get lost on the fold in the map."

"Ask the boss."

"She's doing something to her hair. She's got these electric pliers."

London traffic is a constant emergency. It's a twenty-four-hour crisis. People who come to live here tend to imagine they've arrived at a particularly bad time. Five years later, hunched and battle-hardened in the driver's seat, they might just remember that they're still waiting for things to calm down and get back to normal again. The only way around London traffic is to get to know your own patch and don't stray too far. I'm still getting used to Shepherd's Bush. As far as I can tell it's basically a massive roundabout attached to a motorway. There are four separate shops selling everything for £1 and a kebab shop called the Spice Grills that never shuts, day or night.

We live at the end of a small, neat row of white houses that have sprouted up between the back of the Tube and the edge of a huge building site. Laura has been here for a few years now. The house is still new and well looked after. There are curtains in bright patterns, soft lighting and an incredible number of pillows and cushions piled around the place. Sometimes I come home at night and it takes a few moments to convince myself there's not been some mistake and that this is actually where I live.

"Do you know what Daisy's wearing? I can't wait to see."

Laura has finally emerged looking – but don't on any account tell her this – just as good as she does eating breakfast, going to buy a paper or falling asleep on the sofa.

"Well, she is the bride. My guess would be a wedding dress."

"What colours are they having?"

"All beige. Dick's wearing a beige suit and beige shoes. He's got beige hair. Why do they have to have colours?"

"They don't have to. They might want to. People do."

Dick and Daisy were at college with Dan and me. We don't see each other that much any more, but we're still good friends in the way you are when you all know that you're in it for the long haul: New Year's Eve, birthdays, that kind of thing. Some friends turn into cousins after a while.

Eventually Dan turned up outside in a pointlessly plush-looking hire car. He wasn't alone. The hiring of the car, without warning and probably at great expense, would have had a lot to do with his feelings for the girl sitting in the passenger seat.

"Hi, you guys. My gosh, it's so nice here. You must love living so near the main street."

Bobby is Dan's on-off girlfriend. She's on when she's here

and she's off when she's back home in New York, which is about half the time these days.

"Bobby, hi."

"I was just telling Dan, I'll bet it's really exciting being down here. Brooklyn Heights gets so boring."

"Yeah, it's great. Did you see those people on the green? They like it so much they camp out all the time."

"Anyway, sorry we're a bit late," Dan says quickly. "Laura, you look lovely. We'd better get on the road in a minute, folks."

Dan doesn't usually get flustered. It's just not him. He doesn't have the right kind of face for it. Despite this, there's something about Bobby (what is it with American girls' names?) that gets to him. She has this weird kind of power. Not that it stops him furiously chasing other women when she's not around. Strange, that. I've never really asked him how he squares it in his own head. But when she is here things tend to work in a certain way.

"Okay, you two boys can drive. The girls are sitting in the back where you can't bug us."

Most of the time Bobby looks like a scary new breed of android. She works for the New York office of Dan's bank. I think she might even be his boss over there. She's got the kind of hair you buy ready-to-wear from a very expensive Manhattan boutique. When she smiles her teeth are aggressively perfect. She could be any age between twenty-five and forty, not that it matters. With a certain type of American woman it's as though they've done away with age altogether. Bobby is of course very attractive in an appalling kind of way, like a sporty car you'd be totally flummoxed by if you ever had to drive it.

"Hey. I told you, honey, easy on the brake or no tip. Now Laura, tell me more about you and publishing. When are we going to see you in New York?"

It was a two-hour drive through the semi-detached wilderness around the North Circular. We followed the slow Saturday traffic down an endless dual carriageway until, eventually, the chatter from the back seat seemed to merge into one steady sound.

"England–Macedonia this afternoon," Dan said quietly, as we skirted a giant blue IKEA superstore.

"I've got 18–1 for a 2–1 win, Owen scores first."

No social engagement is ever important enough to obscure the fact that England are playing. Or anyone else for that matter. Every Saturday in autumn, winter and spring thousands of men experience the exact reverse situation of that famous episode of *The Likely Lads* where Bob and Terry spend a day trying to avoid the football score so they can watch the highlights in the evening. On days like today the TV section of any good department store will look more like a pub on a busy Friday night.

The wedding was in a small concrete suburb. We were part of the crowd meeting Dick for warm-up drinks in what would have once been the village pub. As we parked the car and walked in through the doors I got the same feeling I always have with Laura on days like this. I like standing next to her. People get drawn into her orbit. She knows how to behave and the right kind of things to say.

Dick looked wide-eyed and nervous as he came across to say hello. His thick hair was already standing up in a spiral on his crown and his tie was a fretful knot.

"Lads, great to see you, thank Christ you're here. Bloody glad you made it."

"Dick, congratulations. How are you feeling?"

"Fine. Just fine actually," he said, swallowing at least half a pint of lager and wiping his mouth on the back of his sleeve. Men in morning suits and silky neckerchiefs took up a whole corner of the pub. What is it with men in morning suits? There always are a few, and it's always the same few. Where do you even get a morning suit from anyway?

"You brought the girls too."

"Yeah. We tried to leave them in the car but they escaped."

"Hi, Dicky."

"Dick, you know Laura, of course, and this is Bobby."

Bobby had already led Dan across to an empty section of bar, where she was talking to him very quickly. Directly behind her a TV screen showed England kicking off under heavy skies in Macedonia. To the untrained eye Dan's attention didn't waver.

Dick is a man's man kind of man. I suppose I knew that the sight of a couple of women at his pre-wedding drinks might disturb him. Sometimes men just want to be with other men, although I have been trying to avoid that kind of thing. Men are never more like men than when they're with men. And these days that can be a bit of a drag.

Scattered around in among the morning suits there were a few familiar faces. Dave and Tim from college. Dick's brother

Ed. It's a strange thing about old friends. We've only got room for so many of them. They stick around though, and that can be enough in itself. Sometimes your friends are just the people who got there first.

We sat at the back of the church, me sandwiched in between Laura and Dan. I'd forgotten how tiring being a wedding guest can be. The wedding smile appears, but once it's there it has to be held in place forcibly. The first few friends' weddings you go to are quite exciting. A few years down the line, by the time you're close to thirty, you're slightly immune to it all. You get used to the feeling of being an extra in somebody else's big scene.

The entrance of the bride shook me out of it. Daisy appeared at the end of the aisle, flushed and slightly unsteady on her feet, and the air seemed to leave the room around us. You could feel the crackle of excitement. Everybody in the room held their breath. In front of us Dick wobbled visibly as he turned to look. Weddings have changed. I used to like the free drinks, the disco and the girls in nice outfits. These days I quite like this bit.

"She looks beautiful," Laura whispered in my ear.

"England one up, Wayne Rooney," Dan whispered in the other one, slipping his phone back into his pocket. At that moment something stirred inside me, a deep and suddenly quite urgent conviction that, whatever else happened that day, in the middle of it all there was one thing I knew for certain. I'd just lost twenty quid.

Outside on the steps of the church I smoked one of Dan's

fags. We watched from a distance as Laura and Bobby joined the crowd throwing handfuls of rice. Below us Daisy gradually dragged a near-delirious Dick into the back seat of a green Bentley.

"It makes you think," Dan said.

"About what?"

"First wedding I've been to where I've shagged the bride."

"Really? You and Daisy?"

"Years ago. Anyway that's not the point. I've done bridesmaids, sisters, a maid of honour. But never the bride. Maybe it means we're all getting older."

"Don't bring me into your seedy world."

The reception was at a country house a few miles down the road. It was a big, rambling place with gloomy oil paintings on the walls and a huge main hall that opened out on to the garden. In a corner of the dance floor we found another familiar face: Simon, DJ Clueless, a gangling figure even when crouched in the middle of an explosion of leads and plug sockets, lights and monitors. Simon knows Dick from when we were at college. This afternoon he was playing his wedding selection, working an eager crowd made up of the usual game dads and uncles, plus a few of the younger cousins and nieces. Dads and uncles do all the serious dancing at weddings.

"Nice first song."

"It's a wedding classic."

Dick and Daisy danced their first dance to the Commodores' 'Three Times A Lady'. By then Daisy was actually holding Dick upright, until halfway through the final chorus when his legs suddenly found an unexpected energy and started trying to move in all directions at once.

"How can you be three times a lady anyway?"

"You start off once. Then twice. Then three times."

"It's a song about having a sex change. The operation is a three-stage process. By the third stage you're done. You're a lady."

"Have you ever wondered how that works?"

"Easy, I'd have thought. It's a scalpel job."

"That way around, maybe. But how do they make a woman into a man? Where does the old once, twice, three times come from?"

"It certainly is a beautiful song."

"It was. Until a few seconds ago."

"The worst wedding song I've heard of is the girl who asked for the Robin Hood music. That Bryan Adams record."

" 'Everything I do I do it for you.' But instead she walked down the aisle to *Robin Hood, Robin Hood, with his band of men.* Yeah, I think we've all heard that one."

"The merry men. What were they so happy about?"

"Magic mushrooms."

"The merry men were all raging queens. What do you think they were doing out in the woods?"

"So Robin Hood was running a gay, druggy theft ring."

"Hello, boys. What are you talking about over here on your own?"

Alongside Bobby and Laura were Daisy's mum, the eager-looking Mrs Cakebread, and an elderly couple who could easily have been grandparents.

"We were just saying what a beautiful ceremony it was," Dan said, not missing a beat. "And Daisy's looking so lovely. You must be really proud."

Mrs Cakebread beamed in Dan's direction. Sometimes he can be almost too smooth for his own good.

Bobby drove us back. She was the only one of us who hadn't drunk anything. What is it with Americans and alcohol? They either don't drink at all or they're raging alcoholics. It's like eating. You can turn yourself into a monument to hamburgers, or you can survive on a diet of radishes. There doesn't seem to be any middle ground. I sat in the back with Laura, who started to nod off as soon as we pulled out of the car park. Through the window the orange lights zipped past, each one taking us closer to London.

"What did you get them?" Dan asked from the front seat.

"Knives."

"Me too."

Bobby laughed. "You both got them knives? What is it with guys and knives?"

"It's the best present."

"Supposed to be bad luck actually," Laura said sleepily.

"Knives aren't bad luck. Knives are useful. Duvet covers are bad luck. Pillows are really bad luck."

There was a long silence. Laura closed her eyes and started to go back to sleep.

"So when are you guys getting married?" Bobby announced suddenly in her sing-song voice. "You've got to be next in line."

"No. We don't believe in marriage. We're going to live in a

commune. Why get tied down when the world is full of single women?" I said, wishing I'd just kept my mouth shut.

"Uh-huh," Bobby said slowly.

Why is it always me who feels awkward when someone comes out with something like that? Nobody said much for the rest of the journey. Laura and I got out at Putney and caught the Tube the rest of the way home. We were both pretty tired by then. Weddings can really take it out of you.

Like marriage, Sunday football is not an undertaking to be embarked on lightly or in haste, but soberly (or with not too bad a hangover), advisedly and in the genuine fear of turning an ankle or doing in your back. As we queue at the Homebase checkout, I manage to find a convenient pile of boxes to lean on. Laura sits on my knee, causing me only mild lower back discomfort and low-level shooting pains down my right thigh. In front of us a woman wearing a large holey jumper waves a crumpled receipt and argues with the cashier about drill bits.

Outside it's stopped raining and the wind smells unusually sweet as we weave towards the car with our trolley.

"You're right, you know. We should go home," I say.

"Why?"

"Highlights of England–Macedonia."

"Right."

"I'm joking."

"No, you're not."

It feels nice to crawl back home slowly. I'm even happy to

see the rain start to fall again. Rain can make things easier sometimes. Stuck in the endlessly recycling traffic of the Shepherd's Bush one-way system, we listen to the radio and eat mints.

"Yesterday was fun," Laura says.

"It was all right, wasn't it?"

"There is something I want to ask you though."

"Oh yeah?"

She pauses. "It's quite important actually. I'm not sure how to say this so I'll just jump straight in. Will you not marry me?"

"Yes. Yes, I won't. I promise not to."

"And can we never have a huge wedding in a church in the country?"

"Yes, we can't. And Bobby certainly won't be coming when we don't."

"Oh shame. Don't be mean about her. She's a very nice person."

"When you get to know her."

"Anyway. I'm glad we've got all that sorted out."

"Yes. It was about time. Now let's go home and plan our future."

After that the rest of the day seems to fly past.

5
Keith wants a word

Sunday November 29th 2004
Bolingbroke Athletic vs. Real Norbury

Keith wants a word: under normal circumstances this could mean anything. Keith has got stuck on the quick crossword. Keith needs to borrow twenty quid (just until next week). Keith is still in bed and won't be with us for at least an hour. All of these might be likely reasons for Keith wanting a word.

This week, however, it seems to mean something else. Already the game against Norbury feels as though it's destined to be some kind of turning point. The first inkling of this comes with us cruising at a comfortable 1–0 down after twenty minutes, when suddenly Keith starts shouting.

"GET TIGHT, WHITES. LET'S KEEP WORKING. WE'RE STILL IN THIS."

There's a polite silence as the ball trickles out of play and all the way down to the garden fences at the far end of Halfmarshes. Someone coughs.

"COME ON, LET'S PICK IT UP, BOLINGBROKE."

"What does he think he's doing? Apart from making my headache worse," Dan says as we wait in the centre circle, watching Keith run across to fetch the ball.

"Search me."

"He's been like it all day."

This is true. The first real suggestion of something a bit odd going down came much earlier this morning.

"Keith wants a word," Laura said.

It was early enough for a shrug of the shoulders as she handed me the phone.

"Mate." Keith's voice was very loud in my ear.

"What is it? I'm still in bed."

"Just checking you're still on for today."

"Of course I am."

"Good man. Let's try and get down for nine. Have a decent warm-up."

"Keith, I'll see you at 9.30. As usual."

"No worries. Suit yourself."

"Goodbye, Keith."

I suspect that Laura has something planned for this afternoon. I'm pretty good at spotting the signs these days.

Mostly it's the way she says, "Don't forget we're going to see Abigail and Greg this afternoon. I've told them we'll be there at three o'clock."

"No. Of course not."

"You could sound a bit more enthusiastic."

"It's always the same thing. When I say I've been playing football they look at me like I'm mad."

"Don't be silly."

"They don't like me on principle. It's class war. They think I'm a yob with an Armani tattoo. They think I run with the West Ham Head Hunters."

"Stop talking into your pillow. I can't hear a word you're saying. We should get a present for the baby too."

In my experience, your girlfriend's friends have two choices when they meet you for the first time. There is no third way. They can either like you straight away. Or they can instantly disapprove of you. No words need to be exchanged. Disapproval is immediately registered; and then tacitly revisited every time you see one another from then on.

Visiting Abigail and Greg is hard enough. Throw in Baby Alex and you're looking at a major Sunday hazard. Last time around somebody had the bright idea of sitting Baby Alex on my knee. Before I'd had time to express strong feelings of alarm, he'd taken his own steps: holding his breath until, turning purple, he was ferried away to safer quarters by his mum. "He's never done that before," Abigail said, in a way that suggested I'd just inflicted some irreparable harm on her first-born.

"Do we need to get them something again?" I asked.

"We don't need to. It might be nice though," Laura said.

"Always nice to be nice."

"You don't really like kids that much, do you?"

"I believe the children are our future. Teach them well and let them lead the way."

"You know something else? You're going to be late."

When I called around for Dan he was sitting on the sofa with the curtains shut playing *Mortal Danger IV* against fifteen other people on the internet. At his feet there was an ancient-looking empty bottle of wine, several Coke cans, dirty plates and a scattering of fag packets. Last night he told me he was staying in. He'd had a Big Friday. He needed the rest. Actually, despite it all he does look slightly healthier, although that might just be a relative thing.

"So Keith called you this morning. Why would he do that?"

"I've no idea."

"He's never done it before."

"No."

"Weird."

This is something I've noticed about Dan. He doesn't like people behaving oddly. In fact he tends to get suspicious of anyone who isn't exactly the same as they were when he first met them. It can be annoying, but it's also one of the things that make him a good friend. He doesn't change either.

Outside it's been raining steadily for the last three days and London has begun to revert to a pre-industrial bog. In Shepherd's Bush there are pools of water deep underground in the Tube station. The puddles on the pavement around the green have burst their banks and joined up to form rivers and estuaries. Yesterday I saw a pigeon wading waist-deep through an oily lake by the kerb, a French fry clutched in its beak.

The pitch at Halfmarshes turns into a swamp on days like these. It's a toss-up as to whether the game will actually go ahead, a prospect that fills me with a mixture of disappointment and cowardly relief. Playing football in proper mud is like trying to run up a steep hill in a gale wearing every single item of clothing you own.

"What's that smell?" Dan says, putting his fag out in the clean ashtray.

"Nothing. What smell?"

"The smell in here. Are you wearing perfume?"

"It might be the kit bag."

Everybody gets a turn to wash the kit. This week it's been mine. It took a whole morning of hauling damp nylon in and out of the machine. The shirt numbers looked weirdly familiar strung out over chairs and radiators. It was like having the ghosts of the Bolingbroke first XI hanging around in our kitchen. Before I went to sleep I made sure I moved them out of the bedroom, not wanting to wake up the next morning and see Keith, Nev and Dave forming a defensive wall at the end of the bed. Dan is right though. It does smell of something: Laura's conditioner/softener/powder that makes your clothes smell like one of those brightly lit cosmetics counters that you have to skirt round to get into department stores. He winds down the window and lights another cleansing cigarette.

I park in the narrow lane at Halfmarshes just as the rest of the team turn up in convoy. The rain drums on the plastic porch as we take it in turns to point at the sky and shake our heads, watching as the referee frowns down at the mud from beneath a large golf umbrella. Moments later, word goes around. We're on. The game is a goer. Inside, Keith is already waiting for us, looking businesslike as he unfolds his team sheet and claps his hands together.

"Lads, this is Kevin, a mate of my cousin. We've got him for today."

Kevin can't be more than twenty. His face is pink and scrubbed under his thick brown hair, but he's mountainously tall and in his pristine tracksuit he almost looks like a proper footballer.

"Keith got you out of bed for this?"

"I'd love to hear what he's been telling you."

Kevin really is very tall. Even his huge red boots look like they belong to a different sporting universe.

"Kev's a bit useful actually. Played at Brentford youth for a year. He should give us something at the back."

No one seems that surprised by this, as Nev, Dave and Bob take up their usual seats near the hot water pipes at the back of the room. Nev is still damp from his pre-match shower, the roll of his belly almost hanging down to the lip of the bench.

"Pop groups."

"Abba," Bob says.

"Boyzone," Dave adds.

"Cheeky Girls."

"Duran Duran."

"Echo And The Bunnymen."

"Frank Sinatra."

"He's not a group."

"Doesn't matter. Green Day."

"Hot Chocolate."

"Imagination," Dave says after a pause.

"Imagination?"

" 'Just An Illusion', by Imagination."

Around football, on coach trips, in distant saloon bars and damp dressing rooms, time is often killed like this. It's basic stuff: A–Z on a single theme. You can always change the subject when you get bored. Which is usually quite often.

"All right. Tennis players. Agassi."

"Borg."

"Connors."

"Jo Durie."

"Chris Evert."

"I used to fancy Chris Evert."

"Federer."

"Graf."

"Henman."

"Ilie Nastase. Everyone fancied Chris Evert."

"Very short skirts. John McEnroe."

"There aren't any Ks ... Kournikova."

"Does she play tennis? John Lloyd."

"I've seen pictures. She might have had a racket in her hand."

"That's too much information. Martina Navratilova."

Somebody smacks a boot on the wall, sending a little flurry of grit and dried mud across the tiles. The door opens and Lucien appears, a gust of cold air mingling with the steam and the smell of mouldering socks. Next to me Charlie is adjusting the soles of his boots with a shiny metal spanner. Keith stands up on the bench by the door.

"Lads, just a quick word before we go out. Oi! Listen up!"

He's wearing a waterproof jacket with the collar turned up. For a moment he looks as though he's actually tried to dress like a football manager.

"We can beat these today. They're not far above us in the table and it's a fucking swamp out there. With Kevin too we've got a real chance. So let's give it a hundred and ten per cent."

"Only a hundred and ten? I usually go up to a hundred and twenty."

"Also, I want us in a different formation today. We're going to play with split strikers. Simon, you're the target man up front. Lucien, I want you just behind, in the hole. Floating."

"I'm floating in the hole?"

"Yes."

"What if there isn't a hole?

"There's always a hole."

"Keith, shouldn't we practise this first?"

"No time for that. Just get out there and do it. Any questions?"

"What's happened to the kit? It smells weird."

"Sorry. Something in the wash."

"It really stinks."

"I like it," Lars says, smoothing his collar. "It's much softer. I've got very sensitive skin actually."

Outside it's incredibly cold, the kind of cold that creeps under your shirt and scrapes up and down your spine. A freezing wind blows the rain straight into our faces as we tie the nets to the posts. I catch up with Keith by the halfway line.

"Keith."

"Mate."

"What's all this about?"

We watch as Norbury go through warm-up at the far end. A number nine wearing white boots performs a few practice sprints on the harder ground. You've got to be confident to play Sunday league in white boots.

"What's what about?"

"Bringing your cousin."

"He's not my cousin. He's a mate of my cousin. Actually, he isn't even really my cousin, he's my ex Susan's brother, who was engaged to Martin from my dad's work."

"Keith, whatever. The point is, why now? And what's all this about playing in the hole. And giving it a hundred and twenty per cent. This is us, remember. We lose some, we lose some."

"That," he says, smacking a muddy practice ball back into play, "is exactly what's wrong with this team. We need to start getting our act together."

"Are you serious?"

"GO ON THEN. GET FUCKING WARM. YES, YOU. GET WARM," he shouts as a bunch of white-shirted players start trying to hide behind each other in the goalmouth. There's a pause while he scratches the back of his head.

"Just trust me. Give it a go."

"Okay."

"Good man."

Kevin has come in for Nev, who's standing on the touchline wearing a hat, a scarf and a huge padded coat buttoned up to his chin, and not looking too upset at being dropped on the coldest day of the year. Tall and well balanced, Kevin fizzes a ball powerfully out to Lucien in the murky distance near the halfway line.

We line up in formation, stretched in a fragile line across the pitch. Jerome grits his teeth against the cold as he kicks us off. All week I've been looking forward to this. I even had a dream about playing. In the dream I was wearing a new pair of boots that gave me incredible skills, to the amazement of my team-mates who included people I've worked with in various offices and Mr Gomersall from school. When I looked down my boots were purple and yellow, like rhubarb and custard sweets. I don't know what the dream meant. But taking a strictly analytical view, something tells me if I can just get hold of a pair of those rhubarb and custard boots, well, then we'll really see something ...

Playing into the wind is already starting to take its toll. The blue shirts keep the ball. A tall blond midfielder skips away from Charlie and is brought down with a splash by a tackle from Keith, taking ball, player, boots and shin pads.

"WHO'S GOT WHO?" Keith shouts, back on his feet.

"Who's Hugh?"

"Don't take the piss."

We're being blown back by the wind, dragged by the slope to the far corner of the pitch. A low cross comes in from the right. Under pressure I hack at it with my left foot. The clearance screws out to the edge of the box, where it's driven back in, striking a leg and deflecting past Lars in goal. There's a hush as he turns to fetch the ball from the back of the net.

"Come on, lads, for fuck's sake," Keith shouts into the wind.

"Don't worry, not your fault," Jerome says as I walk back with Dan. "Not your fault you're crap. What's wrong with Keith?"

"Generally?" Dan says. "Or just today?"

Keith has got the ball under one arm and he's saying something to Dave that involves a lot of pointing. As the game kicks off again Lucien seems to have taken Keith's advice. He's darting from left to right, slick-heeled in the mud. I forget how good he can be. Low to the ground, he darts into space and feeds the ball inside to Dan. When they're both in the mood for it, the game feels very different.

"One more, one more. Go right," I shout, as Lucien turns and toe-pokes a cross towards goal. Miraculously, as the keeper reaches down to collect it, the ball strikes the thigh of a defender and deflects past him and into the net. We've scored. We mob Lucien from all sides, ruffling his sodden maroon hair.

"Let's go again, lads," Keith shouts, fists clenched, shirt clogged with mud, looking more than ever like a very intelligent gorilla.

And before long we've really started to play. Kevin has turned out to be quick and strong at the back, hoovering up every loose pass and blitzkrieg raid on our goal. It's strange how quickly the balance can change. TV commentators talk about teams having good spells and bad spells, stepping up a gear or killing off the game. Professional players are like expert boxers, pacing themselves and trading rounds. With us it's a street fight from start to finish. It's a brawl in a car park, all slow-motion haymakers and wheezing headlocks. Most of the game passes in a blur. It's only now and then it turns into something more purposeful.

Half-time comes suddenly. Our breath steams the air as we head back towards the soaking pile of bags and buckets.

"Lads, we've made a few mistakes but the commitment's there. Keep that up and we'll win this," Keith says, reaching into a large plastic bag. "Now. This is a bit new, but I want you all to make sure you have a drink."

He produces a large square soggy cardboard package and starts ripping out some plastic canisters.

"What the fuck is this?"

"Glucozone. High intensity sport refreshment," Dan reads.

"Drink it. It gives you energy."

Bob sniffs at his sachet suspiciously. Next to him Nev has already started sucking energetically on the small yellow straw.

"Keith, where did you get this rubbish from?"

"From the cash and carry. It's not rubbish. It's a sports drink."

"It says made in Slovenia."

"Just drink it."

Keith has clearly lost his mind, but it is quite nice to have something to drink. Even if it does taste like cough mixture. As we head back out, Nev is already on his third carton.

Something certainly seems to have lifted us. We pin the blue shirts back for the first five minutes, the wind behind us creating a strange kind of calm after the gasping pressure of the first half.

"What the FUCK was that?" Charlie shouts, as a late tackle lands him on his elbow in the mud.

"Fuck off," a voice replies and the referee lets out a long blast on his whistle.

"Listen, you lot. There are kids in these houses can hear everything you say. Any more of that and you're off."

The game restarts in silence. The word 'fuck' is very important in football. It's the only swear word you hear used consistently. Fuck fits the rhythm of the game.

"Fucking hell!"

"Fucking want it!"

"Mark a fucking man!"

"For fuck's sake pass the fucking ball."

Fuck fills a gap when you're too tired to think. It's often easier to say it than to leave it out. People who rarely swear in their daily life will say fuck constantly on the football pitch. I once played Sunday league with a solicitor who swore under his breath throughout the full ninety minutes, a mumbled commentary that sounded a bit like: "For fucksake f'kin pass the f'kin ball f'kin f'koff out of it."

Fuck is a devalued currency in football. I've only seen a player sent off once for swearing and that was a mix-up. Our old right back John was called for a foul throw and responded by screaming "FUCK OFF!" at the top of his voice, for which he was immediately red-carded. John is Glaswegian. In parts of Scotland *fuck off* also means *fucking hell*. It's more an exclamation than an insult. John was cursing himself. Unfortunately he was also three yards away from the ref and looking straight at him.

It's mainly loud swearing that referees object to, as well as use of any kind of bad language other than "fuck". There is no excuse for employing any other four-letter word. The general attitude is that any fucker who wants to use that fucking kind of language can just fuck the fuck off.

Norbury have started pushing us back. Eventually two blue shirts appear on the left wing, ganging up on Keith. Suddenly they're through on goal, Lars just seeming to lie down at the forward's feet, like a man stretching out for a sleep on the ground. As the ball is dinked in towards the empty net, Kevin dives desperately to his left. With a loud slap the ball strikes his hand and bounces back out into a puddle.

"Ref, for fuck's sake."

"Penalty!"

"He's got to be off for that."

The referee summons Kevin and brandishes a card silently above his head. The card glows deep red against the sky. The ball is already on the penalty spot as Kevin trudges off towards the corner flag, his pink face lowered. The white-booted forward strolls forward and places the ball easily into the corner of the net. Keith marches towards me, his expression dark now.

"Barn, get up and down if you can." He smiles, soaked and bloodshot. "We can still win this."

And he really seems to believe it. In the minutes that follow he takes up positions all over the field: marauding across to fall over on the right wing, then back miskicking in his own six-yard box moments later. After a high, steepling goal kick he gathers the ball from where it's stopped dead in the mud and toe-pokes a long pass forward to Bob, who stretches but can't reach it with his short legs.

"Bob, for fuck's sake, you've got to fucking make that," Keith shouts from behind me.

"Keith, take it easy," Lucien says. "It's just a throw-in."

"All right, all right."

"Say sorry to Bob."

"Sorry, Bob."

Bob smiles pleasantly. "That's really okay."

The pitch has lost all resemblance to a piece of grass by now. There are swells and dips, an ocean of sludge. As full time approaches, Keith makes a final charge upfield.

"Send it," I hear him scream as I play a slithering pass into his path. Already falling over, Keith takes a step too many and plunges forward as the ball bobbles through to the goalkeeper.

"Penalty!" he's screaming, arms raised like a hungry baby in a high chair, teeth white against the mud that almost completely covers his face. "Penalty, ref!"

"Er, Keith ... I don't think it was a penalty," Simon says, helping him to his feet.

Minutes later the final whistle comes in a long, luxurious blast. We stop where we are in the mud and shake hands with everyone: the opposition, each other, the referee. The rain is approaching horizontal by now. It starts to wash the first layer of mud from my knees as I walk back with Dan towards the changing rooms.

"That was good."

"We needed it after last week."

Jerome comes across and puts an arm around both our shoulders.

"Keith wants a word."

"About what?"

"I don't know. He just said a word."

In the changing room the air is thick with steam. We sit on the benches, dripping with mud and rain. Charlie's got grass between his teeth. Nev is still wrapped up in his enormous coat. Keith looks unusually sombre.

"Lads, there's something you need to know. I wasn't going to say anything. But today's already been hard enough."

"Have they offered you the England job?"

"I'd take it. You only get one shot."

"I'm not fucking about. This is serious. Does anyone know how many games we won last season?"

"A few."

"Two. We won two games. Lads, we're in the fourth division this year. These teams we're playing, they're all third elevens. They're scratch teams."

"So what? We don't have to win the league every season."

"No, but you can't keep losing for ever. I looked at the rules this week. The fact is, if we finish bottom this year we're going out of the league. That's it. Finished. Someone else gets our spot."

"So we'll just be a big fish in the fifth division. Big deal."

"There is no fifth division. There's nowhere left to go after this."

There's a silence around the room. I can see what Keith means. Finish bottom, get kicked out of the league. And then what? The league is what keeps us together. We might complain about it; we might hate the early hours, the referees and, quite often, each other. But these are the only things that keep us going.

"So what are we going to do?" Charlie asks. He looks pale.

"We need to start winning."

"How many points do we need?"

"I don't know. There's plenty of other shit teams. Some of them can't even get eleven players out most of the time. You can't be sure, but I reckon one win might even do it this year. Just enough to keep you up."

"One win."

"How many games have we got left?"

"Eight."

"How hard can it be?"

Nobody feels like answering that.

In the shower I find a long stretch of grazing on my shin. There's a deep throbbing in my right knee and, already, that creeping sense of some deep and terrible tiredness. Wrapped in my towel I sit on the bench and listen to the sound of the rain on the plastic roof. The floor is piled with soaking nylon and heat is spreading out from the water pipes below me. Taking everything into consideration, I can't remember ever feeling quite so exhausted.

The end of football. There are times, just now and again, when it doesn't sound quite as bad as it should.

"Barney?"

"Sorry. I was miles away."

We're sitting in Abigail and Greg's living room. As I come to my senses I notice that Laura is standing up holding a glass of something and looking at me with an expression that suggests she has a feeling she may have met me somewhere before, but she can't quite remember where.

"We're going outside to look at the garden."

"No worries. I'll keep an eye on the baby."

Abigail pauses for a moment. This is just long enough to express genuine dismay at everything I might ever conceivably say or do, while on the surface appearing to smile politely.

"Well. Okay. Greg will be back in a few minutes."

The house is a Victorian semi with a long living room at the back and doors that open on to the small garden. There are Chinese carpets on the walls and way too many ethnic cushions about the place to be any good to anyone. Alex is lying on a sheepskin rug. He looks at me as I pick up a tennis ball-sized beanbag from the shelf.

"All right, Alex," I say, kneeling down. "We may as well have some fun."

I roll the little beanbag ball past him and he watches out of the corner of his eye with a grudging curiosity.

"Let's try that again. Remember, keep your eye on the ball."

After a while there's a bit of a smile and a waggle of the foot. A little later it happens. Sticking out a pudgy left peg, by accident or design, he deflects the little yellow ball off the blanket and down towards the skirting board. There's a look of surprise on his face as he watches it go.

"Nice first touch. Now let's work on your right foot."

After a few minutes he's waiting for the ball to come towards him, and watching it with a look in his eye that I'm starting to recognise. It's the kind of look you sometimes see on the faces of people like Keith and Charlie and even Nev.

"Oh. You've found my Nepalese juggling balls," Abigail says as they come back in from the garden.

"I think Alex might be a bit of a footballer. He's definitely got a taste for it."

Without trying to look anything other than devastated by this news, Abigail scoops up the baby and puts him in his bouncy chair. All the while his eyes follow the yellow ball hungrily as it goes back on the shelf. I really could get to like this kid.

6
Success

At our standard of football, winning is by no means everything. In fact, most of the time winning isn't really anything at all. Trying to win at park football is like trying to win at any of the other things people only tend to do on a Sunday morning, like going to church, shopping or watching cartoons in your dressing gown. It isn't really what it's all about.

That's not to say I haven't played in successful teams. I even own some silverware: the Hanley Park Crofton Five-a-Side under-twelves winners' trophy 1986. Silverware probably isn't the right word. It's more like plasticware, a black shield with a shiny gold nameplate and a little ball that falls off and has to be glued back on. My Crofton Five-a-Side trophy has come with me wherever I've lived. It followed me to university. It gleamed among the mildew when I lived in a damp corridor on the wrong side of Brixton. It was there on the mantelpiece in the flat next to Dan's collection of ornamental pub ashtrays. It's on the shelf in the living room right now.

I think the trophy might be the only ornament I've ever owned, apart from a piranha fish I brought back from Brazil, which over the years has tended to sit next to it like a bodyguard. People have sometimes wondered why I still keep it around.

"Why do you insist on keeping that thing around?" Laura asked. We were in the middle of tidying the flat. Or at least she was. So far I'd managed to keep my input down to either nodding agreement or raising a reassuring eyebrow.

"I'm not insisting." I reached up off the sofa and took the trophy out of her hand. "It's just one of my things."

"You know, the glasses my mum gave us would look really good above the fireplace. There's nowhere else to put them."

"This trophy is my greatest achievement. You wouldn't ask Nelson Mandela to move his Nobel Prize because your mum's glasses need some shelf space."

"You know what? I probably wouldn't. But listen, Nelson, mate, can't we put it in the bedroom for now?"

I have to admit, the Hanley Park Crofton Park Five-a-Side winners' trophy isn't particularly nice-looking. It's the kind of thing you see at car boot sales. Twenty pee for the trophy. Okay, go on then, ten. All right you can have it for free if you take those Elton John albums.

"I was in the local paper that week. Top goalscorer."

"You told me."

"I suppose it can go somewhere else. It probably should be in a safe place."

"That's right. It's far too precious to be in here."

"I know what you're doing. Anyway, look how much stuff you've got lying around the place. Explain to me again why we need so many candles."

What is it with girls and candles? They give them to each other as presents. They keep them on shelves. They line them up in rows. Very occasionally they light them. It's the same with girls and flowers. Personally I've got some kind of flower blindness. I just don't see them, even when they're in a vase right in front of me. Even when I'm moving them out of the way so I can watch TV, it's like they're not there at all. This is why men don't buy flowers very often. Most of the time they just don't even see them.

I put the trophy on the windowsill in the bedroom. It does look quite old these days. Twenty years is a long time. In 1986 I was eleven years old and already a widely travelled schoolboy veteran, at least compared to the novice who'd stepped out on to the pitch for Elmvale Primary School. For the last two years I'd zigzagged across a succession of teams. Like someone who's learning to dive, I plunged in again and again. Lethbridge came and went. So did Ladywell All Stars. Eltham YFC didn't last more than two weeks. There was a new rhythm to my life and everyone else had to get used to it.

"Mum, I can't go on Saturday. I've got football."

"Oh yes. Football. Of course."

I was, weirdly, quite quick for my age – weirdly given that these days even when I'm running as fast as I can, I look like I'm trotting after a frisbee or hurrying out to get a paper. Most important of all, I could hold my own in most local teams. So I walked long distances to halls, parks, youth clubs and play- ing fields, coming home with cuts on my knees and grazes on my elbows. Once I wore shorts for three days just to show off a huge anvil-shaped bruise on my knee.

After two years of a journeyman five-a-side existence, I settled at Hanley Park. Hanley Park were different. For a start they were actually quite good. I joined in November and we just kept on winning games. The team was run by some of the parents from my school. They came to watch with picnic baskets and folding chairs and we had proper coaching and a silky blue-and-black striped kit. Playing for Hanley Park was like being part of a big family. Everybody knew who did and didn't get on with each other, but we all mixed and gossiped and shared sandwiches and lifts home. My mum didn't come down to watch. I hadn't ever asked her. Hanley Park were all mine.

There were some familiar faces in the team. My friends from school, George and Chris, played for them. George was our goalie. He had all the gear: green and yellow jerseys, gloves, padded trousers and a big flash sports bag. He took being a goalie so seriously that he rarely wore any other kind of clothes. But Hanley were a serious team, and this was one of the reasons I stuck with them. It wasn't always easy.

Along with the others, there was Jason, who really was trouble. Jason was like an open secret. He was sent off for swearing a couple of weeks after I joined but nobody said anything. People let things go with Jason. Rules were bent and stretched. He was a big kid with very pale blond hair, a jaw that jutted straight out and two small and very dark eyes. He was louder than the rest of us and he had a certain air of menace that all football teams like to have somewhere in their ranks.

The first time I went to Hanley Park Jason made a point of talking to me. He stood next to me the whole time. He almost wouldn't leave me alone. It might have felt like he was being friendly; if it wasn't for the cold feeling I got in my stomach whenever he came anywhere near me.

"Don't worry about him," George said after that first evening. "He just winds people up."

"What do you mean?"

"It's just what he does. He's a nutter."

"Great. That makes me feel much better."

It was a while before anything happened, but I think everybody could feel it brewing. At our midweek practice we used to boot the practice balls around in the corridor before our coach John unlocked the doors to let us into the hall. On these occasions Jason quickly developed a habit of slamming the ball at me as hard as he could. Fortunately for me his game was much more about power than accuracy. The signs were there though. Kids always know. And there was definitely something funny going on. He'd marked me out.

But I still liked being in the team. The other kids were friendly. It was nice getting lifts with George's dad. We'd been winning games and I'd been scoring goals. It was just this one little thing that never went away, the sick feeling when Jason gave me a slightly too brutal dead arm.

It all came to a head one Wednesday at midweek training. We were standing against a wall waiting to be split up into groups for some practice when out of the blue Jason just decided to start kicking me. He was laughing too, in a horrible kind of way, but still kicking me really quite hard. At first I was more surprised than anything else.

"What are you going to do about it?" he laughed, kicking me again. We both knew that the answer was nothing. I didn't have a clue what to do.

So it went on all evening. Kicking, but also a fair split of punching and threats. Nobody said a word the whole time this was happening. A discreet space was maintained around us. Coach John blew his whistle and told us what to do, and basically ignored the fact that I was having the crap kicked out of me. If you've ever been trapped next to the violent drunk on a night bus, with nobody else lifting a finger to help, you'll know exactly how it felt.

Eventually Jason managed to grab hold of my head. Still laughing, he pushed it back hard against the wall behind us. There was a clunk and for a second I understood why people talk about seeing stars. And then I was lashing out. I missed with a punch but, following it up, managed somehow to kick Jason's ankles away from underneath him as he stepped forward. He fell sideways slowly, his head making a wonderful slapping noise as it hit the stone floor. I'm not sure which of us looked more astonished. Fortunately, before anything else could happen, the whistle was being blown again and we were off shooting at cones or dribbling around quoits.

People always say you should stand up to bullies. Show them you won't be pushed around. They'll soon be crawling away with their tail between their legs. Clearly, this is bollocks. In fact, standing up to a bully usually only gives him a greater incentive to use your head as a basketball. This was an important lesson to learn at an early age. If only I'd learned it at a slightly earlier age than that night in the five-a-side hall.

Predictably enough Jason didn't suddenly become a coward, look for someone else to pick on or decide to try and become my best friend. Instead he got really angry. Now it was open warfare. Every week was just about staying out of his reach for as long as possible.

"George."

"What?'

"Don't tell me not to worry about Jason any more."

"He has a go at everyone. He doesn't mean it."

"He looks like he means it. Why doesn't someone stop him?"

"You can't." George shook his head.

"He's a nutter?"

"Exactly."

Twice in the next few weeks I came home with a black eye and once with a bleeding nose. And for a few hours each Wednesday and Saturday playing with Hanbury Park became the coldest, loneliest place in the world.

For a while I became a bit of an outsider. Kids can't help it. They see someone being picked on and they run the other way. They just don't want it to be them having Jason kicking their brown Adidas sports bag across the changing room.

This was how the evening used to start. This was Jason's way of saying hello. I didn't really mind. It was only a bag after all and not my face or anything.

One day, however, things finally did come to a head. It started with Jason punting my bag against the changing room wall again. This was fine. This was normal. Except today I'd made the mistake of keeping a whole carton of orange drink, given to me by my mum, in with my shorts and old sticking plasters and copies of the *Eagle*. As I picked the bag up I could hear liquid sloshing around inside. A trickle of sugary orange drink had already begun to emerge from one corner. Somebody else spotted it and laughed. This, finally, was too much.

"Look," I said. "Look what you've done."

Gurgling with laughter at something else, Jason turned round to face me. He looked a bit surprised. I didn't talk to him at all these days. He'd probably forgotten what my voice sounded like.

"My bag. Look at it." I shook it and some more orange stuff splashed out.

He reached out and grabbed the strap.

"No. It's mine."

I knew what he was going to do. He wanted to turn it upside down, shake it up a bit and then throw it against the wall again. I could see it in his eyes. To be fair, I'd probably have done exactly the same in his position.

"Give it here."

"No. It's mine."

With my left hand I grabbed his index finger and started prising it away from the strap. This was a surprisingly success-ful move. I had the sudden and terrifying satisfaction of seeing Jason turn cross-eyed with pain as I bent the finger, not only off the bag, but right back away from his thumb.

"You'd better stop that," he sneered, but without his usual total conviction.

"No. You stop."

Back went the finger, as he started trying to club the side of my head with his free hand. I kept dodging, all the while tightening my one-handed grip and savouring the terrible thrill of inflicting a totally unexpected pain. By now there was an excited crowd.

"Jason, let him go," George shouted.

"Leave it out."

"Come on, Jase. Stop it," someone else pleaded.

"Get out of it," he snarled back.

If he wasn't going to admit what was really happening, then neither was I. Jason was still flailing at me with his fist as I tightened my invisible grip. In the middle of my delight at this turn of events I couldn't help feeling slightly disappointed that nobody else could see what was happening here. Thanks, I felt like saying, I really do appreciate your concern, but I seem to be actually winning this round.

After what seemed like about ten minutes of grappling, John finally arrived, just as Jason's finger was running out of space to be bent back into.

"All right, boys, let's have you outside. Come on then. Five minutes."

In the confusion we separated. Around us everybody else sat down and got back to getting changed. In a corner I emptied out my bag, drinking what I could of what was left at the bottom.

Jason didn't come near me for the rest of that night. It was the same the next week. And by then an unspoken truce had descended. That's another thing about kids. Generally, they always do forget after a while. And soon I'd almost forgotten about Jason. A few weeks later he gave me a sweet while we were waiting to be let into the five-a-side hall. Nobody else noticed it, but something significant had passed between us, and it wasn't just a strawberry Mojo.

In the end it was football that kept me and Jason apart. The fact is, he wasn't really that good. He was more of a team bruiser, a mascot almost, and Hanley Park were too ambitious for that to last. After a while his place was taken by Sammy. Sammy was Vietnamese. Not only did he fill a Jason-shaped hole, he was stocky and skilful and incredibly strong on his feet. We were already pretty good. Sammy would become our secret weapon.

That spring we arrived at the Crofton Five-a-Side hotly tipped. In its time the Crofton Five-a-Side tournament was the largest off-season under-twelves five-a-side competition in the SE23 area of London. That year. Probably. It was held in the main arena at the Crofton Park Leisure Centre, a large wooden-floored hall with a balcony and a tiered row of seats.

Crofton Park is a South London backwater, not quite the middle of nowhere, but definitely an outpost on the way there. The streets unfurled in rows of terraced houses, with a cluster of shops and a shuttered pub every five hundred yards. There were other things too: a lumpy, mouldering cemetery and a bus garage that always seemed to be empty apart from one abandoned single decker. And of course, once a year, there was the Crofton Five-a-Side.

The competition was held over school half-term. For the final day the hall was packed. I played in attack in front of George in goal. This involved scuttling about in the furthest part of the pitch and shooting whenever I got the ball. I can still remember some of the goals I scored, usually with the help of Sammy and Angelo, my striking partners: a toe-poke into the top corner of the aluminium goal, and a shot on the turn past the keeper who sat staring at the floor after the ball had gone through his legs.

It's a rare feeling playing in a successful team. It's like running downhill. Suddenly everything just starts to go your way. We knew we were going to win every game. The opposition were nothing more than a degree of resistance that would eventually be worn down. It was only when we reached the semi-finals that for the first time we started to feel nervous.

"Look at all those people. It must be a thousand," George said as we peered through the door into the main hall. The seats were full and the balcony was a mass of faces.

"More than that. Five thousand," I said.

"How many thousand in a million?"

"There might be scouts there. From Millwall."

"Brownies more like. They might take you."

I've never been any good at standing up and performing. In our annual school nativity play I'd been cast as a pig, a sheep and an envelope. This involved standing totally still with my arms stretched out, wearing a white sheet. Even in my final year, when everyone got a speaking part, I was cast as a passer-by who gave the three wise men directions and then went away very quickly.

This was different. We had something people wanted to see. We'd practised together. We knew each other's strengths and weaknesses, and we knew exactly how we were going to win. Now our success had become public property. We even looked like a team when we weren't on the pitch. It was 1986 and even primary school kids wanted to dress a bit like someone out of a Levi 501 advert. A platoon of junior casuals, we emerged from Cortinas and Fiestas wearing market-stall clothes and with haircuts that had begun to stray from the childhood bowl towards a creeping fringiness.

We won our semi-final easily. Afterwards the whole team sat together with coaches and parents as we waited for the final to start. A respectful space was cleared around us. Food was brought and picked at. George sat with his goalie gloves next to him on the table. I had a tracksuit top, which I wore zipped up to the neck, feeling like somebody guarding a precious strength. Even Jason was there, at the far end of the table sitting with the parents.

"Just go out there and play like you have all week," John told us, and we didn't even really need to listen. The hall was brightly lit and the crowd formed a wall of noise around us as we squeaked and thundered around the varnished floor. I don't remember exactly how we won the final, just the realisation halfway through that we would, the strength in my legs born out of relief. The trophy was presented on a platform in front of the gallery. Cameras flashed and there were cheers and handshakes. We stood together in the middle of all the mums and dads and brothers, not wanting to break ranks.

Afterwards we sat at a table in the bar drinking long cardboard cups of Fanta. My socks were rolled around my ankles. I thought of the footballers I'd seen on TV, the FA Cup winners holding pints of milk. Angelo jumped up on the table and had to be persuaded to get down. A team that had become a weekly source of agony only a few months ago now seemed closer than had ever seemed possible.

In fact, at that moment it felt as though everything was exactly in its place. How often do you get to feel like that? Obviously it's easier when you're eleven years old, before you've learned that triumph on the five-a-side pitch isn't really that big a deal in the scheme of things, and that the world is shot through with compromise and the occasional plea-bargained success.

I came home with my Crofton Five-a-Side trophy in my hand. A few days later my mum brought it back with my name engraved on the front. She'd taken it to the shop on Deptford High Street just down from the place where we bought my first boots. I put the trophy by my bed. At the time it felt like this was just the beginning. Medals, cups, gongs, ceremonial platters. This was how it would be from now on.

In fact I've still only got the one. People have laughed at the plastic trophy on my shelf. It has been interpreted as an ironical gesture. Laura wants to move it into the bedroom and then, ideally, to somewhere even further down the chain like the shelf in the toilet or the cardboard boxes wedged under the bed. I used to think it was a bit of a joke myself. I'm twenty-nine years old now, and I'm not quite so sure any more.

7
Being professional

Sunday December 5th 2004
Sporting Leatherhead vs. Bolingbroke Athletic

Something bad has happened. Something even worse is about to happen. And something really terrible is pencilled in for the afternoon. Beyond that it's all a bit hazy this morning. Either I'm getting older much too quickly or, when I do go out in the evening, I'm drinking much more than I used to. Or perhaps both. My head feels as though it's been injected with some poisonous liquid. There's a ringing in my ears that, after a moment's investigation, turns out to be the alarm clock. Using a hand that feels like a bunch of bananas attached to my wrist, I manage to fumble it into silence.

Even by recent standards I'm looking pale. In fact, my skin seems to have turned light blue. In the bathroom mirror my teeth are an unusual mustard yellow. At least they've got a bit of colour in them. Once, when I was living with Dan and before I gave up smoking, I found myself cleaning my teeth with steel wool. That was a particularly bad morning. Now I think about it, the shredded grey fuzz was still on the rim of the sink when I moved out.

"Are you all right?" Laura asks.

"Fine. Fine."

I'm not sure this is a question designed with just my physical well-being in mind. Laura has been up for a while. She hands me a cup of something I know might make me feel better, if only I could raise it to my mouth and drink it.

"What time did you get in? I must have been asleep."

"Oh, not that late."

"I was back at twelve."

"Probably just a bit after that."

"How was everyone?"

"All right. We got some things sorted out."

Last night was a Bolingbroke council of war. After Keith's news last week we decided it was time for a proper team meeting. It turned out Saturday night was the only time we could all make it – not ideal preparation for the start of our winning streak, but it was always going to be a quiet one. We ended up meeting in a new bar in Brixton, a place being opened that night by a mate of a mate who knew someone who knew someone else, who was vaguely acquainted with someone who happened also to know Dan and Simon.

"Just tell them you're with me," Dan said, as we walked straight past two bored-looking men in bomber jackets and up two flights of stairs to what turned out to be a dingy, low-ceilinged bar. Keith was sitting at a table with the Hawk.

"It's a bit loud in here for a team meeting," I shouted above the music, as Dan handed me two small white pieces of card.

"Drink tickets. First night," he said, heading off to the bar. At the table Keith was drinking what looked like a fruit salad upended into a pint glass and decorated with a straw.

"Free drinks," he shrugged, beckoning as Lars and Charlie appeared out of the gloom. Before he could sit down the Hawk had leaned across and crushed a fistful of tickets into Charlie's hand.

"While you're up. Six lagers, a double vodka and whatever you want."

"Who are we missing?" I asked.

"Bob's not coming," Jerome said. "He goes to bed at nine o'clock. And Nev's late."

"Nev is coming here?"

"This is his big night out."

Keith and the Hawk were already deep in discussion.

"Chewbacca is Han Solo's dog," the Hawk was saying noisily. "He can't speak. He just barks."

"He talks all the time. How else does he fix up the ship?"

"He roars. That's not a proper language. You never hear anybody roar back at him. They've learned how to understand his noises. Like a dog."

"If he did speak a proper language," Keith says thoughtfully, "C-3PO would know about it. He's a translator droid."

"Chewbacca isn't a dog. He's Han Solo's gay lover. It's one of the great screen romances."

"I don't even want to think about that. Imagine the sex."

"At least they're having some."

"You don't need it, mate. Everyone knows scoring a goal is better than sex."

"I wouldn't know. I don't have much experience of either."

"It depends what kind of goal and what kind of sex.

Last-minute equaliser, winner from thirty yards, good sex, bad sex ..."

"A pissed-up one-night stand when she's twice your age and her husband's asleep next door," Dan suggested. "Then again, David Trezeguet at Euro 2000, comes on in the final and scores the winner from twenty yards. He'd probably say that was better than sex."

"Better than the worst sex he's ever had."

"At least as good as wanking."

"Lads, before we get too comfortable," Charlie said, speaking above the music. "Can we get down to what we're here for?"

"What's that then?"

"What Keith said last week. We need to start taking things seriously or the team isn't going to last much longer."

"Is it really that bad being kicked out of the league? Can't we just find another one?"

"There aren't any that will have us," Keith admitted. "And how many of us have got the energy to find something else? If Bolingbroke folds, that's it. Football finished."

Charlie looked pale at the thought.

"That's a bit over the top isn't it, Keith?" Jerome said.

"Not for you. You're twenty-five."

"Six."

"Whatever. If we go under it's early middle age for the rest of us."

"So what do we do?"

"Play better. Win. I don't know."

There was a long silence.

"We could always get Terry back," Dave said.

Someone laughed. Terry, our one-time captain and team manager, hasn't played for us for years. Not since his sudden abdication. Just the thought of him is enough to make most of us feel more than a little bit uneasy.

"We're not that fucking desperate."

"All right. It's just a thought."

Suddenly there was a disturbance near the door. Above the heads of the crowd I caught a glimpse of a bulky, red-faced figure, who seemed to be bundling his way past the two security guards. Nev was wearing a sports jacket; jeans that may well have had creases ironed into them and squashed brown leather brogues.

"Can you believe that? They almost didn't let me in. Right. This place is crawling with birds. Who's drinking what?"

"That man over there is one of our team-mates," Dan said, as Nev bumped his way towards the bar with a fistful of drinks tickets. "Just in case you were thinking this is going to be easy."

Today we're playing Sporting Leatherhead. It's a long drive down the A3, a road that's a racetrack of white vans and veering sales reps even on a Sunday morning. Where do all these people come from? And why aren't they at home asleep? Dave's Volvo can fit four across the back seat, provided two of them are Jerome and Lucien, and as long as Nev is in the front. I've got Simon's elbow in my ear, a child's car seat on my lap and a selection of toys rattling around my ankles. From the driver's side Dave hands around a paper napkin full of small pink cakes.

"We had a birthday party yesterday. One of the perks of parenting."

"Did you make these yourself?" Dan asks, biting off a small corner.

"Yes. With little Jamie too."

Dan stops chewing and balances the rest of the cake on the back shelf. I can't help it. I get some kind of mild dyslexia whenever people start talking about their kids. It brings on a complete mental block. I know I'm not alone in this. But whereas Dan, for example, doesn't really care, I am actually interested. Up to a point. I just can't ever think of anything to say.

"How are they?"

"Nice. Moist inside. Crisp on the top," Nev says, chewing slowly.

"Not the cakes, the kids."

Dave looks at me in his mirror.

"They're fine. Just learning how to break things."

There's a long silence, broken only by the sound of Nev eating his way through another fairy cake.

"We're nearly there. This exit. Quick."

Dave swerves across two lanes and off the dual carriageway. At the end of a succession of roundabouts that leave us all feeling a bit queasy we find the Leatherhead ground, a large expanse of grass with a single pitch in front of a row of silver birches. It's a crisp sunny day and the far end of the field is dusted with a faint mist. There's a pause while we all wait for someone else to move first.

"This is it," Jerome says. "Start of the winning run."

"My head hurts. It's not even a headache. It's my whole head. And my hair too."

"Maybe we should stay in the car."

"We can't do that," Dan says firmly. "Charlie might see us."

By the time we clamber out the windows have steamed up and the inside of the car smells a lot like a pub around closing time. My feet are already soaked with dew as Dan rattles open the door to the changing rooms.

"Here's the bin men," Keith says. Several pale, disconsolate figures are seated on benches around the edges of the room. No one has managed to get changed yet. There's a loud sneeze behind me. A gangling presence, wearing size fourteen boots, Simon seems to be quietly crying to himself in the corner.

"You all right?"

"Yeah. I'm fine."

"Sure?"

"It's nothing, really," he sniffs. "Just these contact lenses. You haven't got any eye drops have you?"

We change in silence, the air heavy with hangover. I notice Charlie has carefully polished his boots.

"Lads. Just a moment," Keith says, calling us together. "Last night wasn't exactly ideal preparation. But we know what we've got to do today."

"Get some sleep. Drink lots of water," Lucien suggests. Slumped against a radiator, he hasn't opened his eyes yet.

"We've got to be professional. Let's keep it nice and simple. We're playing with a diamond midfield for this one. Charlie, I want you in front of the defence. Jerome, in behind the strikers."

"How's that a diamond?"

"These two go right and left," he points at Lucien and then at Dan. "It's a diamond shape."

"What if I go over to the other side? What if I have to drop back? It won't be a diamond any more."

"Doesn't matter."

"We could end up with a triangle."

"Or a hexagon."

"Just stick to the diamond. And leave the jokes to me. Remember, we're being professional. Now I've got some bad news. Lars can't make it today. He's not feeling well. Someone's going to have to go in goal."

Keith looks around blankly. Somebody coughs. Dan laces a boot.

"You can't be serious."

"We don't stand a chance without a proper keeper."

"I'll do it," I hear myself saying. "For a half anyway."

I dig in the kit bag and find a goalie jersey that looks as though it's got a collection of sweet wrappers stuck to the front. There's also some huge gloves that smell of ancient compost heaps.

"Wear these. They're padded."

Keith throws a pair of skin-tight black tracksuit bottoms across the room. Reluctantly, I stretch them over my shorts and then follow the rest of the team out into the watery sunlight.

The pitch is dry and crumbly, but with a soft underside. It steams gently as the sun creeps out of the mist, creating delicate pink patterns in the clouds above the far goal. Feeling like an early morning eccentric in my multi-coloured top, black padded bloomers and oversized gloves, I catch a couple of practice balls and watch another zing into the top corner.

"Make it yours. Command your area."

"Stay big. Don't go down too early."

"Don't look so fucking gormless."

From my goal I've got a wide-angled view of the two teams as we line up for kick-off. The opposition are in orange. It's a terrible kit: tangerine shirt, black shorts and black socks. The two forwards lining up to kick off look dangerously rangy. There are signs that mark out the proper footballer. There's a twitchiness, a looseness in his limbs. There's definitely something about these two that signals danger. Probably it's the way that, from kick-off, the one on the right barrels straight towards our defence, jinking past a couple of tottering figures in white before being hacked down desperately by Keith. I clump my gloves together.

"Heads up! Turn and face!"

The free kick is taken quickly. There's a menacing gathering of orange, and suddenly I'm bounding out to block the ball with my feet and seeing it loop out towards the edge of my area. Without thinking I charge through the crowd, punching one-handed like a child chasing a balloon. The ball flies straight up in the air, and I leap after it again, batting it out of play on the near side.

"Commitment, keeps!" Keith shouts, and someone laughs as, feeling like a circus act, I skip back towards goal. Charlie seems to have taken it on himself to be everywhere at once today. Straight-backed and short-legged, he pops up on the left wing behind Lucien. Moments later he's back on the right next to Dave.

"Well in, Charlie," someone shouts as a tackle sends the ball spinning away over the far touchline. You've got to hand it to him. He may take it all far too seriously. He may still live with his parents. And he may, quite possibly, possess a large collection of hand-painted mail-order souvenir china plates. But he really does care.

"Get there. Make sure. Well in."

"Got to want this, boys."

Being in goal you do a lot of shouting. I can't remember the last time I really yelled; not in an open space, at a group of people who are completely ignoring me. Still, it's Keith's voice that seems to be gathering strength as the half wears on.

"Channel it," he shouts in front of me. "Find the pass," he adds, as Nev hoofs the ball aimlessly out of play near the touchline.

"Bend your run," Keith is telling someone now. "Stay alive. Read the play."

"What's he on about?" Jerome asks me, as we wait for the orange shirts to fetch the ball from beyond the trees.

"I don't know. I think he's being professional."

"He sounds like he's been watching too much Sky Sports."

"Mark space! Pressurise the ball carrier!"

I used to play with a man called Harvey who shouted, "GO AWAY!" whenever he got the ball. "Go away" means give me room, make a run, get down that wing. Shouting, "Go away" is okay, as long as you only do it now and then. Harvey used to shout, "Go away" whenever he had the ball. Even when someone else had it nearby, he'd be barking, "GO AWAY!" at anybody who crossed his path. He just had a deep need to shout, "Go away". But better that than turning into one of those men on the top deck of buses who talk in a loud voice about having their phone tapped by the CIA.

Twenty minutes into the game we pause for breath briefly. As always, this turns out to be a terrible idea. Finding a huge hole in the middle of our defence, the orange shirts surge through the space and suddenly the rangy centre forward is bearing down on me.

I rush forward, thinking about making myself big and forming a barrier and staying on my feet, and all the other goalkeeping guff. Pausing to look up, the centre forward lifts the ball out of my reach and past my left hand, as I realise I'm standing miles too far over to the right. I make a scrambling attempt to claw it away, but only succeed in catching my boot in the bottom of the net. It takes a few moments to untangle myself.

"Come on Bolingbroke. Nil–nil now," Dave shouts as I toe-poke the ball towards the centre circle. Except it isn't. It's 1–0. And it's all starting to feel a bit familiar.

I take a couple of goal kicks and manage to find decent distance, remembering to aim for a space, rather than just blindly hacking the thing as far as it will go. Just as I'm starting to feel good about things, my third kick trickles out of the penalty area to the feet of the orange-shirted number nine, who only misses scoring by a combination of his surprise and my own war dance on the edge of the box.

"Careful, keeps. Make sure."

Yes, make sure. The next time I get my hands on the ball I sprint to the edge of the area and thrash it as hard as I can, hearing the hum as it streaks over the halfway line, yards ahead of the nearest player.

"Kick, keeper," comes the shout from the touchline, as I prance around self-consciously in my black bloomers. Almost immediately, the half-time whistle blows. I follow the white shirts towards the halfway line. As I get there I feel a tug at my elbow.

"Come on then. Let's have 'em."

It's Keith, keeping his promise to go in goal for the second half. Whipped by the chilly wind, we swap shirts.

"Nah. I can't wear that." He holds up the green and purple goalie top. "Makes me look like a porn star."

From the kit bag he produces a plain black silky shirt with padded elbows.

"That's more like it."

The goalkeeper on the other pitch is a huge man in bright white socks. Even from fifty yards away he fills the goal like an upturned sofa or a small van. He catches the ball one-handed, like a sea monster crushing a sailboat in its paw.

"Look at the size of that keeper. How are we supposed to compete with that?"

"You think you feel bad now, wait 'til you see him in the showers."

Sunday football is an exhibitionist pursuit. Legs and guts and arses are all up for comment. It's no place for the insecure. Steel yourself before entering the changing rooms if you have a single long strand of hair scraped across your scalp, or if you're still in denial about your burgeoning beer gut. In a football team there's nowhere to hide.

"Listen, lads. Forget about what's gone on out there. You," Keith gestures at Lucien, "think he's not covering, then say something. But I'm not having us going at each other. This is supposed to be a team. What are we?"

"Shite."

"One–nil down."

"We're professional."

We stand around in silence. Nobody makes any bad jokes. No one even complains or asks if there are any aspirins. Charlie looks pale and slightly tearful. Even Keith seems weary.

"What's it going to be, then?" Dan says.

"What do you mean?"

"We have got a choice you know. We can either try and do this together. Or we can all find something else to do next year."

The words hang in the air as he turns away and has a drink from a bottle of water.

"Nice one," I say, going to stand next him. "You really cheered everyone up there."

"Yeah. I thought so."

"Why does Keith keep talking about bin men?"

"Don't you remember? Last night."

"Not really. The last thing I remember is the Hawk telling me he could have most of the newsreaders on TV in a fight. Even the ones who come on a bit hard, like Peter Sissons or John Humphrys."

"Paxman could be a bit tasty."

"He's confident he could take Paxman out if it came to it."

"It might not though."

"No."

"So you don't remember the rubbish bags."

"I think I do actually."

It was all to do with those drinks tickets. After a while I found out where the Hawk was getting them. The tickets were just pieces of card printed with the name of the bar. It hadn't taken him long to realise the logo was on every menu, flyer and beer mat in the place, all of them just waiting to be cut into shape with the penknife on his key ring.

After three hours of free drinks, a shortage of raw materials led me and Dan to go foraging in one of the back rooms next to the kitchen. Inside a pile of plastic bin sacks we found not only a single soggy menu, but a whole load of other rubbish that spilt out all over the floor and just wouldn't go back in. And then suddenly a strong hand was on the back of our collars leading us out of the small room, through the bar and back on to the street. The soggy menu was still in my trouser pocket when I woke up this morning.

"Straight in, Bolingbroke," Charlie shouts from the centre circle, a hint of menace in his voice as Bob and Simon kick us off. There is something different about us now. For a start, we're all running around like a bunch of desperate single men in a disco half an hour before chucking out time.

"Defend from the front," Keith shouts, as Simon tries to nick the ball away from an enormous orange-shirted centre half. He stops suddenly, quickly enough to send Simon bouncing off his backside and over into the mud.

"Well in, Si. Stay on your feet," Charlie shouts as we press in behind him. And in a ragged way we are starting to get somewhere.

Jerome nicks a short pass through to Bob, who executes a slow motion silent movie turn in the penalty area. The nearest orange-shirted defender chooses this moment to fall over sideways, leaving him with a clear path to goal.

"Shoot! Shoot!" Jerome shouts at his shoulder. Bob stops and turns towards him, a smile playing on his lips as he thinks of something to say.

"Not now, Bob. Just shoot."

With the air of a man uprooting a thistle among his tomatoes, he turns and side-foots the ball decisively into the corner of the net.

"GO ON THE WHITES. BOB, YOU BEAUTY, WE'RE BACK IN THIS," Keith shouts from behind me.

"Who's the man?" Jerome shouts, holding up a palm for a high five.

"I don't know. Is it me?" Bob asks, shaking the hand politely.

With the score back to 2–1 I'm starting to wonder for the first time. Could this really be it? No one really seems to know for sure. Pushing forward a few moments later, something looms in front of me, almost blocking out the light. It's the giant centre back, a six feet five inches tangerine colossus. His thighs bulge. His ankles also bulge. So do his feet. Lunging in like a gladiator prodding a lion with his trident, I nick the ball away, feeling a paunchy expanse against my elbow.

"Well in, Barn! Use it now," Keith shouts as I pass sideways to Lucien, who runs straight for goal. Dipping a shoulder he scurries past one man, beats another and is knocked sideways by a third.

"Referee!" Keith shouts.

"Football, Lucien."

"Why doesn't he do that more often? Is it just me? Or could he do that more often?"

Lucien slinks away towards the far side, rubbing his hip. It's a free kick just on the edge of the penalty area. This might well be our last chance. The referee waves the orange wall back ten yards and waits with whistle in hand as a Bolingbroke conference forms around the ball. First Keith has it. Then Dan takes it and places it on a patch of clean grass, before being overruled again by Keith.

"Lads, when you're ready," the referee says. Finally a familiar figure emerges from the huddle. I've hardly noticed Nev today. Skulking at left back, he doesn't seem to have immediately taken to our newly professional regime. Taking a deep breath he rumbles towards the ball, gathering momentum like a landslide. The wall has begun to quiver. Stuttering suddenly, Nev loses his step but swipes a big, fat boot at the ball, catching it a glancing blow.

The shot gets no nearer goal than Nev himself in his follow through. Falling like a roadblock in front of the opposition defenders, he starts to scramble back up to his feet, taking handfuls of orange shirt.

"Good effort, Nev."

"Get up, for fuck's sake."

In the confusion he wrestles back possession. Wound up like a gigantic toy mouse he shuffles towards the ball again, but this time tap-tackles his own ankles and plunges forwards, sliding goalwards on his stomach.

"Go on, the big man."

"Bury it," Jerome shouts. As Nev comes to rest the stationary ball is nicked away from the end of his nose and cleared upfield finally.

"It's not fucking funny," Keith shouts as he dives in for a tackle near the halfway line. All around me players on both sides are either chasing the ball or bent double with a mixture of exhaustion and asphyxiating giggles. Charlie has to dodge Jerome and an orange-shirted bystander in the centre circle as the ball breaks loose. Even the referee looks wild-eyed.

"Be professional," Simon wheezes as Nev creeps back towards his hiding place at left back. This is a new departure for us. We've been a joke before on the football field. But we've never really been a *joke*.

By the time the final whistle comes we're ready for it. We troop off together in resigned silence. In the changing rooms a warm mist has begun to creep out of the showers.

"Well, that seemed to go quite well," Bob says, sitting down.

"Could have been worse."

"You are joking?" Keith says, hurling a flag into the corner of the room. "You try to do things properly, try to start putting it together, and you end up more useless than you started. Lads, we've got a lot of work to do."

"Did you see my free kick?"

"No, Nev. I must have missed that one."

"I nearly nailed it. I had it for a second."

"What you nearly had was a heart attack."

Keith scratches his head. "I mean it. After this we need some ground rules. No more hangovers for a start."

"Well, whose fault was that?"

"All of ours. No more mucking about either. No more taking the piss when the captain's talking to you."

"Let's not set our sights too high."

"No more soft touches. We need some bite."

"What do you mean?"

"For a start, I'm bringing the Hawk out of retirement."

"Oh God. He'll be getting Terry along next. Don't get Terry along."

"I'm serious. From now on we take no prisoners. This team is getting nasty."

8
Trials

I'm not sure if playing football teaches you to live with disappointment. It would be nice if it did, but the evidence suggests this might not be the case. The playing fields of the South London Sunday leagues are not filled with placid, well-rounded individuals. There is no glow of lessons well learned, of acquired wisdom and shared resilience. Or if there is it tends to get lost in all the fighting and swearing.

Football may not teach you to fail better but it certainly teaches you that success only comes around very rarely. And that, when it does, it tends not to last very long. Here's an example: in 1993 Tottenham defender Pat van den Hauwe and Mandy Smith were football's faces of the moment. That summer the game was in a unique state of excitement. Money from the first deal with Sky TV had begun to slosh around and suddenly football was everywhere, in every pub, bar and house that could afford a huge fungus-shaped satellite dish. Hyperinflation was in the air and everybody was promised a piece of the pie, through wages, advertising or extra-large brown envelopes under the table at the motorway service station.

Football was hungry for somebody to throw all this new

money at before it burned a hole in the pocket of its best pair of rayon-mix club slacks. A carnival king and queen were called for. Into the glamour vacuum stepped the faces of the moment, the game's newest celebrity couple, and the subject of a seventeen-page spread in *Hello!* magazine: Pat and his bride Mandy. The wedding was a front-cover splash.

Pat was a tough-tackling left back in the late stages of his career. For the benefit of *Hello!* readers he was rebranded as "one of the world's top footballers" as well as "the world's most romantic man", a claim that remains difficult to disprove without any hard evidence. Mandy ("one of the world's most beautiful women") was a professional model and had previously been married to Rolling Stone Bill Wyman. Pat, on the other hand, had formed a defensive partnership with Derek Mountfield and Kevin Ratcliffe at Everton. It was a meeting of glamorous worlds, the start of ten years of intermarriage between football and fashion, and a prototype for the Beckhams themselves.

Unfortunately it was also a disaster. Within six months stories had begun to circulate. Pat and Mandy appeared in the tabloids denying stories of late-night shouting matches outside their London flat. There were rumours of bust-ups, the resurfacing of an eating disorder and the unravelling of Pat's career at Spurs. Tales also emerged of his fondness for dressing up in Mandy's clothes, the defensive hardman going so far as to walk the streets disguised as a woman. Then came the death knell: separations, a moving out and eventually the divorce.

Pat is living in South Africa these days, no longer one of the world's top footballers but possibly, for all I know, still hanging on to his title of most romantic man on the planet. Mandy is still around, still appearing on television, still in the glossy mags talking about how much better off she is these days. It seems likely that she is happier too, now she's got the urge to shack up with aged bassists and hard case full backs out of her system. Predictably it was Pat who, at the time, seemed to have come out of the whole thing the worse for wear.

Footballers have a difficult life. Leaving school before time, they emerge briefly in their early twenties before finding themselves ushered into retirement at an age when most people are thinking about getting a proper job. Even for those who do make it, being a footballer is shot through with disappointment and missed opportunities, beyond which the entire professional game is constructed from the failure of thousands of young men to do what a few hundred manage with only fleeting success.

Six months after Pat and Mandy had exchanged their vows a story appeared in the *Sun* under the headline THE BOYS WHO DONE GOOD! Catching the spirit of the times, the paper had identified a group of fresh-faced young prodigies, the footballing millionaires of tomorrow. "Eleven mates from one small school have been snapped up by top soccer clubs," it revealed. Posing in the colours of their chosen clubs, the eleven wannabees from the Dartford West School class of '93 smiled and clenched their fists in anticipated triumph.

Five years earlier and it could have been me. By 1993 I was already thinking about going to university. When I was fourteen, however, all I wanted to do was play football. When you're fourteen it seems – for a little while – as though it might all go on for ever.

"Your mum wears army boots."

"Your mum's so old she took her driving test on a dinosaur."

"Your mum's Hitler and your dad's a penguin."

"Mercedes. That's mine."

Dan pointed out of the window as a red car passed on the other side of the road. We always sat on the top deck of the bus. Either the front seat or as close to the back as you could get. What sort of person sat on the bottom deck anyway?

"Your mum," he said slowly, "*is* your dad."

"That's rubbish."

"It's wicked. It's the worst."

It was Saturday morning and we were on our way to football. Bus to London Bridge, train to Brixton, then bus to Herne Hill. It usually took at least three hours there and back. When you're a kid you don't seem to mind that kind of thing.

"Let's go to McDonald's."

"We haven't got time." Dan looked at his new watch. He was always looking at his watch.

"Yes, we have."

"We'll go in Brixton. Porsche. That's mine."

A couple of older girls squashed into the seat in front of us. We sat in silence for a moment.

"Where's your friend?"

"Simon. He can't come."

"Your imaginary friend."

"Shut up. He just can't come."

Dan had been threatening to bring Simon from school for about six weeks now. Not that Brockwell Park FC needed new players. We were a decent junior team. By a roundabout kind of route Brockwell Park had grown out of Hanley Park. Football teams spread out like family trees. Hanley Park was born out of Elmvale, Lewisham Star came from Hanley Park and some of the kids from Lewisham, me included, moved on to Brockwell. Dan came from school. He came with me.

"So what happened to Simon?"

"His dad said he can't go today."

"Why not?"

"I don't know."

"Is he scared?"

"Scared of what? You?"

"Dan's got an imaginary friend."

"Is your leg all right?"

Expertly he punched the top of my thigh, using his knuckle to drive deep into the muscle. It was a textbook dead leg. Nobody knows more about the precise biology of inflicting pain than a teenage boy.

"They reckon there's going to be Charlton scouts today."

"Don't get excited. Neil said they watch Norwood every week. They're top of the league. They've got some wicked players."

"They're still coming though."

"Everyone said they were coming before. They never did."

Dan put an Opal Fruit in his mouth. He offered me the packet but, seeing it was a red one, took it out and let me have the green.

"What about tonight?"

"What *about* tonight?"

"The party."

"We're not going. It's Jack's party."

Dan had been going on about the party at our house all week. It was for Jack's birthday, his seventeenth. Outside of home we didn't see each other very much any more. I didn't really like his friends. Most of them were older kids from school who either acted cool or ignored you. Some of them, even worse, were girls.

"Don't be gay. It's a party. He won't mind."

"I mind."

"You're chicken."

"I am not."

I pretended to look the other way as the girls in front stood up to get off. With Dan turned towards the window I flicked him hard on the earlobe. One of them laughed as she went down the stairs.

"That's raw."

"Unlucky. Very unlucky."

Down below us shop windows flashed past, a train appeared between the terraced roofs and the traffic lights changed to green up ahead as we started to rumble forward again. It was a gloomy day. Rain spattered the windscreens and the trees looked bare and brittle even though it was only November. At London Bridge we jumped off at the lights with our bags and boots and ran for the platform. It was still an adventure in those days to be travelling around on our own.

Nobody has ever been so swift with their train times or so ready with their tickets. The train creaked south over main streets and zebra crossings and past back gardens that appeared briefly between the scrubby trees. We tended to talk less on the train. It was more public than the bus somehow.

"Millwall," Dan whispered, as two men in blue football shirts sat down at the far end of the carriage.

On Saturday afternoons we mixed with the football traffic. We'd heard, and then retold, all the stories. Once someone's brother had been hung out of the window all the way to Victoria. There was talk of the Millwall smile, a long scar at the corners of your mouth from a slit with a knife. In truth I'd never seen anything remotely like this. No groups of skinhead boot boys had ever pounced on us. We'd never even been stared out. But still we sat in silence the rest of the way. You never did know.

Football was different in 1988. The people around it were a lot more frightening for a start. In the wider world Kevin Keegan had long since retired into ancient history. Super Kev had been replaced as leader of the national team by Captain Marvel. Bryan Robson's superhero status sprang from a habit of hurling his fragile body around the field with psychopathic abandon. He was harder to like than Keegan. He was square-jawed and dour. That summer I watched on TV as England lost every game at the 1988 Euro championships. Robson was grim-faced and morose. Later, I'd realise that silent suffering was his natural facial expression, probably as a result of a heavy session the night before with fellow Old

Trafford Drinking Club members Paul McGrath and Norman Whiteside.

In more ambitious moods there was Glenn Hoddle. Hoddle was sophisticated. He was elegant. He wore his socks around his ankles. Now and then he scored spectacular goals and played fantastic passes. Dan fancied himself a bit of a Glenn Hoddle. There was just enough arrogance about him to get away with it. Some of the kids at Brockwell hadn't taken to him at first. Dan, of course, had barely noticed.

At Brixton we ducked through the ticket barrier, skipped around the drunks outside the station and cut though the crowds towards our bus. The ground was at the far end of Brockwell Park, a sloping field open to the wind on all sides until they built a tall fence to stop the ball bouncing all the way down to the road on a breezy day.

It was at the end of a long path away from the main road. Walking from the bus stop you got a long-distance view of everyone who was there ahead of you. As we got closer I could see George already in his goalie kit talking to Kerry, a kid from around the park who also used to play for Hanley Park. George hadn't really changed much since primary school. Not as much as I had anyway.

"All right, Barnsley."

"All right, Georgia."

He still looked like the same fair-haired kid, just taller and skinnier. George had had good instincts about hanging on to his goalie jersey the whole time. He'd grown enough in the last two years to loom a whole head above the rest of us.

"All right, Danny boy."

"All right. Where's C-3PO?"

"Not around. He was here."

Our coach and manager was called Neil. We called him C-3PO, mainly because of the way he walked. There was something in his voice too. Teenage boys can be cruel, but they're pretty much always right on the money.

George and Kerry weren't the only ones still playing from our Hanley Park days. There was Angelo too and sometimes Sammy, who had gone from being a sturdy eleven-year-old to an increasingly mountainous teenager. Things had started to change when we left primary school. We were all at new schools now, but nobody was at a school quite like mine.

I'd been given a free place at the posh school across town. It wasn't easy at first. Kids just want to fit in and I wasn't any different. My voice began a rapid makeover from mangled south London to an imitation of public school. It settled down after a bit. By now it had stopped halfway: posh at first hearing, but listen out for the odd slip here and there. It's pretty much stayed like that ever since. Playing for Brockwell Park had become somewhere we could all meet, an in-between place. I'd brought them Dan too. In the end everyone likes Dan.

Inside the changing room our shirts had already been hung up on our pegs and our shorts and socks were neatly folded on the bench, sure signs that Neil had been here already. It takes a certain kind of person to run a kids' football team.

"Over here. Oi, Georgina."

George was going through his warm-up routine. This

involved repeatedly throwing a ball against the far wall as hard as he could and catching the rebound. He'd heard something about Peter Shilton doing the same thing when he played for England. The wall at the far end had already begun to disintegrate in several places.

"Oi, give it here."

"I'm warming up."

"You going to get spotted today?"

"Have you heard about that? Someone's meant to be coming down."

"No one's going down. Just Kerry's mum."

"She can't make it. Her wooden leg gets stuck."

"She was coming but they only let her out at the weekend."

Our other central midfielder, Gary, had arrived by now. He was a nice, quiet kid who'd missed most of the season with various injuries. He sat down next to Dan, who was eating a packet of crisps.

"All right, Gaz. They coming for you?"

"I bet he's had more offers than you'll get."

"Only from your sister. And your dad."

"Good morning, everyone. Nice to see you here early for a change."

Neil wore tinted glasses so you could never be totally sure whether he was talking to you. His hair was neatly parted and slightly lank and his chin seemed to taper away into his neck. He'd been wearing the same plastic tracksuit trousers and grey cardigan every time I'd seen him for the last two years. We all went back to getting changed. Dan put away his crisps and started strapping on a shin pad. Neil, whatever else he may have been, was still the boss.

"Now, we're playing a good team today. I want you all to work hard for each other and do your best out there."

He reached into his pocket and produced a small notebook.

"Here's the team. George in goal. Steven, Christopher, Alexander, Barnaby defence."

"Yes, boss."

"Don't get cocky, kid."

"Kerry, David, Daniel and Edward midfield."

"Yes, I'm centre mid."

"The force is strong in this one."

"All right. Settle down. Up front Richard and Michael."

"Go on, the Brockwell."

"Shut down all garbage grinders on the third floor."

It was just habit with us by now, but Neil still didn't seem to have twigged our routine of trying to fit as many quotes from *Star Wars* as we could into every team talk. Not that it would have bothered him. Brockwell was his club. It had been his long before any of us joined. It probably still is his for all I know.

I jogged across towards the pitch with Dan.

"What about the party then?"

"No. I don't know."

George was pacing around in his goal, marking out his angles. In the centre circle we formed a wide arc and started doing our warm-up exercises. Brockwell Park is still the most disciplined team I've ever been in for warm-ups, warm-downs, keeping your position, playing to the whistle and all the other little things you're supposed to do. Give them the right kind of rules and kids tend to stick to them.

The game, in the end, was just another game, another one of the hundreds, it seemed, that we'd played together. As always we started at top speed. The need to ease yourself into it only comes later in life. Norwood were a good team. They had three or four bigger kids, bigger than us anyway, who ganged up on us in midfield. Despite this we started well. Dan hit a post with a shot from the edge of the area and Ricky, our centre forward, had a couple of good chances that he put wide.

I was still in the middle of my love affair with tackling. All I wanted to do was launch myself across the grass feet first, particularly on a sticky pitch like the one at Brockwell, which always had a soft top and mossy grass. Sometimes I even dreamed about tackling.

One early slide sent the ball over the touchline and all the way down the hill to the trees. I had a good look around while we waited for it to come back. There were the usual familiar faces watching from the shelter of the tall fence. Neil was standing very still in his raincoat. Along from him were the opposition manager and a couple of people who looked like coaches. Some parents, a passer-by or two, a kid on a bike and in the distance a couple of policemen on horseback. No one looked like they were taking notes.

At half-time the score was still 0–0. We sucked the juice out of our orange quarters, probably the only fruit or vegetable any of us would willingly eat all week. Nothing tastes quite as good as a half-time orange when you've got mud in your mouth and your lips are dry from forty-five minutes of wind and shouting.

Neil talked to us a bit about picking up and tracking back, but mainly we ran up and down to keep warm and kicked a ball around between us. Half-time in those days was just when you were told to stop. Tiredness didn't really come into it. Later there would be a point, in every second half, where goal kicks would start to fall short and at the back we could scarcely clear the ball beyond our own penalty area. Every team had at least a couple of kids for just these moments, kids whose only real skill was being able to hoof the ball much further than anybody else. We had Kerry. Kerry really could boot a ball.

The second half was just another second half, apart from one thing. Maybe it was all the talk of scouts and trials. Maybe it had something to do with my brother asking me if I was going to be a professional footballer in front of one of his friends and then laughing as though that was the most ridiculous thing. For the first time I really noticed Gary in midfield. Everyone knew he was good. He was quiet too and he'd been injured for so long. He wasn't a leader or even particularly popular. But he could do things that were different.

First he picked up the ball, swerved away from three Norwood players and hit a shot that grazed the bar. Then he turned in midfield and played a long, perfectly curled pass out to Ricky on the left. He had a way of running, a light-footed glide. Watching him made me feel as though I was actually standing still. And right there I had the feeling, for certain, that

I wouldn't be the one who kept on doing this. It wouldn't last for ever. People are made differently. Gary had something; not obviously at first, but just enough to let you know you didn't have it.

There are plenty of ages in life where you're supposed to grow up. You turn sixteen or eighteen or twenty-one and things are meant to feel different. If you play football these cut-off points happen all the time, moments where people around you start to move at a different speed. Suddenly there's just nowhere to hide from it.

We ended up losing the game 2–0. Norwood scored twice in the last five minutes. They were better than us, and bigger too. We didn't mind losing. At the end we walked off in a thunder storm. The adults on the sidelines, the coaches, parents and spectators, all scattered off to the safety of the dressing rooms as the rain hissed in the mud around our feet. We didn't mind the rain either. It was nice to be out there in the open, dripping and muddy and on our own.

It never took us long to get changed. By the time we got outside again it was just starting to get dark.

"Boys, make sure you go straight home," Neil said as Angelo and Ricky wrestled in the doorway over half a Marathon bar.

"The force will be with you. Always."

"Don't hang around. I had phone calls last week."

It was gloomy under the plane trees on the main road. We dodged through the teatime gridlock, the streetlights reflecting orange on the wet pavement. In Brixton we stopped in a group for chips from the Chinese fish shop on the corner.

"No vinegar. Just salt please. Lots of salt. More please."

"Where's the red sauce. This is brown."

"It's ketchup. Not red sauce."

"It's tomato sauce."

"What's the difference?"

"I don't know."

"Taste it. Then taste that. It's exactly the same."

"Mister, this red sauce tastes like brown sauce."

"And the brown tastes like red."

"You boys go now. Thank you, bye."

We stood in the street with our chips, feeling the cold begin to bite at last as the sun disappeared behind the flats on the other side of the road.

"Ricky, you know what you could do?"

"What?"

"Start your own chip shop."

"Screw you, Daniel."

"Me, Richard? Screw me?"

The bus back home always seemed to take much longer. Probably we just talked less. Going home we'd see football shirts in the crowds again but it was less exciting this time. Like us, everyone was in a hurry. Going home was never as good as going out.

"Dan, what are you going to do?"

"Now? I'm going to your party."

"When you're older."

"Be rich."

"Is that it?"

Dan nodded, very serious suddenly. "I'm just going to be rich. What about you?"

"I don't know. Be rich as well," I said doubtfully.

"No chance."

"You'll be something else. Like a teacher."

"Right. That's it."

With the flat of my hand I hit him hard as I could between the shoulder blades. There was a deep echoing sound from inside his chest. A woman in front turned and frowned at us.

"Ah, man. That's raw."

Things did change after the game against Norwood, but not for a while. For me Brockwell Park lasted another year or so, which isn't bad for a junior team. We never found out if there were any scouts around that season. Maybe some of those Norwood lads are playing in the Premiership now. Either way, I never did have any schoolboy trials. I was never cut from a prestigious youth team. I was never the unknown teenager in an oversized blazer, sandwiched into the academy photo between Archie McNab, future England captain, and the legendary Sprockington brothers, whose fame and wealth I consider every morning during my milk round. None of these things ever happened.

But something like it did happen to Brockwell Park. Gary, our midfielder, did get spotted. He stopped playing for us a few months later and started training with Crystal Palace. We couldn't believe it at first, but someone's brother who knew his brother said he'd been going down there every weekend. At the time we thought that was it for him. He'd be on the TV before we knew it, playing in the first division, maybe even for England.

It didn't work out like that. Come to think of it, I never heard of Gary again. Maybe he made it somewhere. More likely he became one of the thousands of kids who take the first step then fall out of the system somewhere along the line.

What about those stars of the future, the *Sun*'s THE BOYS WHO DONE GOOD? It would be nice to report on their palatial homes and mahogany trophy cabinets a decade down the line. Of the lads in the line-up Sam Keevil (age twelve, signed by Chelsea) would have a spell at Basingstoke, while Adam Morrish (age fourteen, signed by Queens Park Rangers) played for Dover for a while. The rest just vanished from the game. What remains is a snapshot, a clutch of gawky grins and a moment that captures all the hope and beached dreams that keep the game afloat.

The fact remains that somebody always does succeed. That same week the papers carried a story about a thirteen-year-old who had attracted the attention of Premiership clubs through a display of keepy-uppy in a McDonald's advert. Scouts were queuing up to talk to Scott Parker, a little boy with bobbed hair juggling a ball that looked bigger than his head. Parker would later sign for Charlton and go on to play for Chelsea and England. His success might not seem like such a big deal, if it wasn't for the failure of the boys from Dartford West and all the others who've gone down the same path.

One thing did happen. We did end up going to the party. We started off at Dan's house. In his room we plastered our hair with gel.

"Check it out."

"This stuff stinks."

"It's cool. Chicks love it."

"Yeah right. We'll see."

After that Dan changed into a shirt that was too big for him, we drank a few cans of Coke for energy, and before long there was nothing else left to keep us from going there.

"All right, dudes. You look tough."

Jack opened the door. He had a drink in his hand and he was talking to someone over his shoulder. He seemed pretty friendly, but all the same we slipped in under his arm before he could say anything.

Inside, Dan's bravado seemed to have taken a knock. We sat on the sofa feeling low down and very small as Jack's friends listened to Pink Floyd and pretended to be more drunk than they were. Kids who I'd only ever seen in school uniform were lounging in our kitchen and smoking cigarettes. Groups of impossibly sophisticated girls shimmered together in the corners of the room.

"Hey, you shouldn't be drinking beer."

"Cool shirt. Shame about the hair."

Eventually a couple of very tall and very grown-up-looking girls took pity on us.

"What's your name? I'm Dan."

"I'm Emma and this is Sarah and we're much too old for you two."

"Not that much. What have you done to your foot?"

"I've sprained it. How did you know that?"

"I can tell by the way you were walking. You should rest it. Sit down."

At times like these Dan has always had something special about him. Take him to a party, take him anywhere in fact, and somehow he always knows the right thing to say. The other girl, slightly smaller and blonder, turned to me.

"Have you noticed anything?"

"Nothing I could tell you about."

"What's that supposed to mean?"

"I … don't really know."

"Are you going to blush? He's going to blush."

Smiling, she reached up and pinched both my cheeks. Dan laughed behind me. Not sure whether to laugh or just run away, I settled on grinning. It had definitely been a day for surprises.

9
Things get ugly

Sunday January 9th 2005
Real Norbury vs. Bolingbroke Athletic

I've never been in a proper fight. Not many people have. This is probably because, in order to have a proper punch-up like the ones you see in the movies, you have to be able to fight *back*. It's like playing football: there are people who can do it and people who can't. You need to have some moves, or a grasp of the basic techniques, before you even start thinking about punching, head-butting, or throwing someone through a plate glass window with one hand.

Above all it takes practise. Fighting is difficult. It's also really frightening. Like me, you've probably been threatened, jostled and occasionally hit. If you're a man it's unavoidable. It goes with the territory. But actually having a fight? No chance. Not if I can help it, not while I've still got a pair of half-decent legs to run away with.

On the other hand, I have regularly fouled, kicked, knobbled and tripped. Playing football I've had my fair share of rumbles, most of them governed by the unspoken rule that neither of you is going to take this any further than a slightly firmer than usual handshake at the end of the game.

Sometimes it does get out of hand. Once, playing for Black

Horse Rovers the season before I joined Bolingbroke, I had a proper scuffle with a player on the other side. It didn't get much further than a couple of punches, followed by the shock, not totally unpleasant, of being hit, and then the relief of our team-mates holding us back while we both pretended to try and get at each other. We were pretty polite for the rest of the game, although it was about ten minutes before I realised my lip was bleeding all the way down my shirt.

Some are more fragile than others, but every team has its breaking point. By the time most of us were eleven years old Hanley Park had become a bit of a tasty team. We knew it too. Mainly this was because we had two enormous kids in our side, Kevin and Kerry, who dwarfed not just every other under-twelve we came up against, but most of the dads, coaches and referees too.

We used to travel to games in a minibus, all of us wearing our blue and black strip and feeling ready for a ruck as soon as we turned up. It was around this time that Angelo's graffiti habit emerged. For years afterwards I'd see his name on walls and bridges around Lewisham and Deptford. Back then he used to tag up every place we played at. Once we drove into the car park for an evening match and saw the words *Hanley is big and bad we mash you up* already written in foot-high letters across the wall of the main hall. There was nearly a riot on the spot. We won, of course.

That's just how it is sometimes with football teams. The bonds are loosened. It's a different kind of atmosphere, one without women for a start. And without women life becomes a football match. It's an off-licence, a urinal, a bunch of eleven-year-olds on a minibus pulling moonies out of the back window. And it's always worse when you've got something to prove.

In the last few weeks, Keith has let us all know what's expected of us. "We've got to fight for this," he told us. "We've got to dig deep and come out of the trenches all guns blazing."

"Keith, it's not a war."

"It is, though."

"No, it's not."

"Well, what else is it?"

"All right. Yes, it's a war."

Today we're playing Real Norbury. It's an away game at Kingswood, another turning off the great concrete estuary of the M3, into the fringes of green that mark the border of Surrey and London. The ground is at the end of a small private road in the middle of a row of houses. It opens out into a shock of grass and sky that makes me blink after the narrow streets. The pitch is set in a huge triangle of open land, bordered by the clubhouse on one side, a spiky hedgerow on another, and the flyover at the far end silhouetted against the edge of the sky. Cars zip along and glint into view above the siding.

The clubhouse is a large Victorian building, red-bricked and ruggedly maintained. Inside it smells musty and well used, heated to the point of claustrophobia by huge cracked radiators that hang like giant ribcages on the walls.

Despite the fighting talk, no one else has turned up yet. I sit in my car and eat a Jaffa Cake. An open-backed builder's lorry has parked nearby. The driver is devouring a very large packet of crisps very quickly. As I watch he upends the bag and pours the entire contents down his throat, before screwing it up and wiping his mouth on his sleeve.

It has been a strange week. Laura found me in the kitchen early this morning. I'd already read the Sunday paper and I was considering making my third pot of tea.

"What's going on?" she asked, after yawning at me for a full minute.

"Nothing. Breakfast."

Women eat strange things in the morning. Deliberately passing over the toaster and the packet of thick cut Wiltshire back, she began to put together a mixture of yoghurt and dried fruit.

"I don't know how you can eat that stuff. Don't you get hungry?"

"It's nice. You can't have ketchup with every meal. Listen, are you all right?"

"I'm fine. Why wouldn't I be?"

"You were awake for ages last night. I thought you might be anxious or something."

"In America ketchup's a vegetable. Anxious about what?"

She sat down next to me with her bowl. There's something about a girl in pyjamas, even early on a Sunday morning. You just can't argue with them.

"I don't know. The team. It can't be easy thinking about stopping. I know how much you all rely on it. It's hard to move on."

Most things I can put up with. You can say what you like to me. It's like water off a padded Umbro training jacket. But sometimes people are just so wide of the mark you have to say something.

"We're not giving up and no one's moving on."

"No, of course not. But you might do."

She carried on eating breakfast, choosing a really bad moment to start reading the Style section of the paper.

"We just need to focus. Get our heads down. Concentrate. Stuff like that."

It took longer than usual to pack my stuff. No one should get up early on a Sunday morning. You feel slightly confused for the rest of the day, like you've put your head on inside out. By the time I was ready to leave Laura was sitting on the sofa in the living room watching a programme about sheep farming. She looked up as I came in, both hands around a mug of coffee.

"Listen, I'm sorry," I said. "And it's no big deal. Really, I'm fine."

She looked up at me and blinked for a moment.

"Okay. That's good."

"Good. That's that then."

"I was just trying to say I'd understand if you were worried. Football keeps you all together. It's kind of why you're friends."

"We do plenty of things together. Not just football."

"I can just see you and Keith walking around art galleries."

"We might do."

This is the kind of thing you come up against when you play football. I don't normally mind. It's just today, what with not sleeping that well and Sunday morning and everything else.

"And by the way, you know you really shouldn't eat fatty foods before you exercise," Laura called out as I left the room.

"Talk to my nutritionist."

Pre-match food has always been a touchy subject. Liverpool manager Bill Shankly insisted his players eat anything but red meat before a game. He even sent spies to snoop on the snacks they ate on train journeys. A badly timed ham sandwich could put you in the reserves. Another manager kept his players to a regime of just one bread roll each at lunch. He used to count the rolls afterwards and demand to know who had eaten any that were missing. I used to play with a centre forward who had breakfast at half-time, a large tea and a hot dog from the snack hut just down from the far pitch on Blackheath, and only started to play at about 11.30. Generally scrambled eggs on toast don't seem to cause too many problems. Best of all you can actually force most of it down on a Sunday morning without immediately wishing you hadn't.

By now both teams have arrived, Bolingbroke in a familiar convoy of cars. We're crowded into the dry heat of the dressing room, fighting for space by the radiator. Bob is wearing woolly gloves, which he carefully tugs off his fingers and rolls into a ball. Dan arrives with Simon and dumps his bag next to me in the corner.

"The only reason I used to live with you is that big heap of a car. Two of us in his Mini. It's a joke. Simon, you're six foot five. Get yourself a proper motor."

Simon smiles and carefully folds himself on to a corner of bench.

"Where's Keith?"

"That sounds familiar."

"He'll be here," Jerome says, removing his hood to reveal another hood and, eventually, just his headphones. "I spoke to him yesterday. He's got something planned."

No one seems excited by this prospect. Keith has had things planned before. The team dinner in a kebab shop on Tooting High Street. The night out at a table-dancing club, which ended with the rest of us relieved to be refused entry, while an aggrieved Keith was being bounced down the stairs in a half nelson by two doormen.

Next to me Lucien changes out of his black trousers and black jumper and pulls Bolingbroke kit over his black underwear and black socks. His hair is black. So is his nail varnish.

"You ready for a fight today, Lucien?"

"Ready for a fag and a coffee."

"Black?"

"White with two sugars. Why?"

Suddenly the door is rattled open. It bounces back off the door jamb, crashing into Keith's foot as he attempts to stride in purposefully behind it. Carefully, he hurls it open again. The Hawk follows him inside.

"Right then."

"So I said to her, acupuncture? I can do that. It's just needles."

"How hard can it be?"

"Right then. Here we are." Keith rubs his hands together.

"Listen to the skipper."

"I am. He keeps saying right then."

"Don't take the piss."

"SHUT UP, FOR FUCK'S SAKE!!" A pulse beats in Charlie's jaw.

"Charlie, thanks," Keith says quickly. "Right then. Everybody ready? Lads, just a few words before we go out."

Gradually the noise around the room dies away. Keith takes a deep breath and adopts a thoughtful pose. By the time he actually speaks we're all listening.

"Right. It's all down to us now, boys. We're not doing this for anyone else. We're doing this for the team. And no offence, any of you who don't fancy it may as well leave right now. Lads, it's FA Cup Third Round day today. If we get a result now you'll always remember it. Whenever Third Round day comes around you'll be able to tell your mates, that's when we turned over Real Norbury.

"It's all about us in here now. This band of blokes, this half-fit bunch of chancers. Any of you gets a knock today I'll personally drive you to casualty. A day like today, you'll just run it off. And everyone else out there who's not turned up, dropped out or let us down over the years, is going to be gutted they weren't here doing a job for us on FA Cup Third Round day."

There's a cheer as Keith finishes and suddenly the mood in the room has changed dramatically. The ref pops his head around the door.

"Lads, the oppo are outside getting warm."

"We're on our way."

The sun has climbed enough to cast a faint shadow, bringing out the patches of marshy green in the ground. Norbury are standing inside a toy-sized set of goals in the distance. The wind picks up the further we get from the dressing room until it's blowing a constant gale right down the length of the pitch.

We form a huddle by the halfway line. We've never done this before but it feels like the right thing to do. Charlie has gone almost totally white. He looks ready to explode. Jerome is jittery on his feet, already eyeing the opposition. Even Bob has adopted a stern expression. His beard twitches darkly. Only the Hawk seems unchanged. He's always up for a fight.

"Three words," Keith says. "Commitment. Courage. Belief. And no going back. Fuck it, that's about seven. Just get out there and give it some."

We separate with a shout. The ground has a rutted feel, like thick clay, and up above us the sun is a bloodshot tangerine in the white and blue above the far goal. As we kick off I've got a nervous feeling in my stomach that I've not had before a game since my debut for Lewisham Star under-thirteens in Bermondsey park in front of five parents and a pair of Alsatians.

Norbury are in green shirts and white shorts. They're a mixture of ages. Their left-winger, closest to me, is in his mid-thirties, squat of leg and thick of neck, but from the moment he picks up the ball it's obvious he can play. And in central midfield they've got an enormous mountain of a man, pyramid-shaped in his bulging shirt, with thighs like sacks of sugar.

"Well in, Jamroll," someone shouts as he swats Dave away and scuffs the ball sideways to no one in particular. I get a good early touch near the halfway line, cutting inside a green shirt and looking up for a pass.

"Send it now," Jerome screams from the left.

"Time, Barn, bring it."

"Man on."

Suddenly I'm being propelled through the air, just long enough to think to myself, yes, that was definitely a slithering sound behind me. As I fall on my shoulder I feel a set of studs nuzzling into my ribs.

"Ref!"

"For fuck's sake."

Tackling is one of life's great pleasures. Throwing yourself feet first through the mud at another person, there's not much to beat it. Being tackled, on the other hand, isn't so much fun. At least you always know straight away whether you're still intact. I get to my feet just as a clutch of white shirts arrives and before I know it we're all in each other's faces. An enraged Keith is leaning over the chunky left-winger, who's still flat on his back on the ground.

"Keith, it's fine. Leave it."

Immaculate in black, the referee prances across and raises a sprightly palm. Eventually we separate and the game kicks off again, but we've lost our rhythm and suddenly we're defending in a narrow line on halfway. The ball travels under the wind like a quarterback throw, skimming off the top of Keith's head as he falls backwards, and into the path of a scampering forward.

Four strides take him clear. I'm sprinting back as Lars stands twitching on the edge of the area. The ball is flicked wide of his grasp and another touch leaves it nestling gently in the baggy orange net. We're 1–0 down.

"Come on, lads. Heads up."

I pat Keith on the back as I walk past.

"It's the wind."

"Fuck."

"We'll have it second half."

"Fucking right we'll have 'em."

"No, the wind."

"Whatever."

Moments later we're on the attack again. The ball is cleared towards the halfway line. As Lucien brings it under control and skips forward a huge green mass looms across his path. It's Jamroll. As Lucien skips to one side a heavy knee sends him sprawling to the ground.

"What was that?" he says, rubbing his thigh.

"SHUT YOUR FUCKIN' MARF!"

Jamroll's voice is hard to exaggerate. When it comes to speaking, Jamroll rewrites the rulebook. Not only does he rewrite it, he throws it out of the window. But only after he's torn it up first. Lucien scrambles to his feet, which doesn't bring him any closer to making eye contact.

"You nearly took a piece out of my leg."

"Bollocks," Jamroll mutters, losing interest as he catches sight of Keith behind him.

"Oi. Go on, fuck off out of it," Keith says.

"WHO FUCKIN' ASKED YOU?"

Short and square, Keith stands his ground as Jamroll lumbers closer, just long enough for the referee to appear between them at a girlish skip.

"That's enough, you two. Free kick whites."

"All right, boys. Straight back in."

We're spoiling for a fight now all over the pitch. Within seconds of the restart Dan has started hacking away at the back of a green-shirted player's legs, like a lumberjack felling a small tree. Fortunately the half-time whistle saves us from any major explosion. The Norbury players look slightly bemused as we jog across towards our pile of bags and coats on the far side. We gather in a close circle. Lucien toe-ends a bottle of water away.

"All right, lads, listen up," Keith says. "There's a chance this is going to get tasty. If it does kick off, I want us to keep close to each other. Don't get caught off guard and watch your back."

"Keith ..."

"Whatever you do, don't go down. Stay on your feet," the Hawk adds.

"Aren't we supposed to be trying to win this game?"

Keith waves me away. "Let's help each other out. When it goes off we're all in there together. As a team."

"Great speech earlier by the way. Where did you get it?" I hear Dave say as I tuck my shin pads back inside my socks.

"It just sort of came out."

"Like Terry at his best," someone says but nobody really wants to think about Terry. I catch Nev's eye for the first time today and he gives me a tight smile then turns to talk to Jerome. Which is slightly odd behaviour, given the slightly odd thing that happened this week.

It was Wednesday morning. I was working at home when Nev called. It may have been the first time we'd ever spoken on the phone.

"Barn."

"Hello?"

"Nev here."

"Nev. How are you?"

"Fantastic. Bearing up ... Okay I suppose. Can we talk?"

"Sure."

"Not like this. Let's hook up."

We hooked up near where I work in one of those identical corporate coffee houses. Curious more than anything, I sat at a table in the corner to wait for Nev. Next to me a group of people were talking in sign language. The women were doing most of the signing while the men took it in turns to nod. How do you eavesdrop on a sign language conversation? Sneaky sideways glances seemed to be the best way. There used to be a deaf pub on Upper Street in London. It got pretty crowded but it was still a very quiet place for a drink.

Eventually Nev turned up. He looked tired, but when he saw me his usual broad grin returned.

"I'll get them in," he said.

"Just tea for me."

"Come on, have a skinny decaf-a-latte. I love this place."

"I don't. Just tea thanks."

"Why not?" Nev looked surprised.

"It's all just packaging. Coffee and cake, what's the big deal about that? It's bog water with cinnamon. Whipped cream and a biscuit for a fiver. In fact if you're buying you can get me a large cinnamon bog water."

"One cinnamon bog water coming up."

By the time Nev had eased back into his chair, removed his coat and answered his mobile ("tell them I said two hundred tuna") I was starting to wonder what we were actually doing here.

"So then," Nev said, toying with a small shortbread finger. He carried on grinning at me. And then suddenly his face fell. People's faces are often described as falling. Nev's really did, like a collapsing marquee.

"I needed to talk to someone," he said. "I hope you don't mind. I thought about trying the others. But I knew I could count on you."

"The others?"

"The team. It's different with us though. We've always had that," he waved a hand, "bond between us. Our little chats."

I briefly racked my brains. Nev once told me about a sexual encounter while he was in the army in Kuala Lumpur. I'd sat next to him in the pub plenty of times. We both used to smoke.

"The thing is, it's Janet."

It turned out Mrs Nev had gone off on an extended shopping trip of European capitals, leaving Nev to run the business, cook his own breakfasts and rattle around their five-bedroom mansion in North Sheen. This was six weeks ago, with no sign of her since except for a couple of messages. Apparently she's started saying "ciao". At least the kids are away at boarding school, but not for much longer.

Why was Nev telling me all this? Because of football. It's been five years now, five years in the same team. Who else do you see for three hours nearly every Sunday of your life? Maybe your family. Maybe, but only if you're lucky.

"You guys, you've always been there for me. I've never really appreciated it until now."

"Well. You know."

"I mean it. Always."

"On a Sunday morning."

"Worst part of the week," Nev said quietly.

"I suppose so."

"Things used to be so simple. Now it's all falling to pieces at once. I can't force her to come home. We'll work it out, God knows how, but we will. The thing is right now I need football, I need those Sunday mornings."

Nev looked at me hopefully. Beyond his usual Sunday morning cheerfulness, I realised he was basically a complete mystery to me. Five years in the same team and when it mattered I had nothing meaningful to say to him at all.

"Have you told Jane how you feel?"

"Janet."

"Janet. I'm sure she's just having a wobble. Women must have them too."

"Yes. You're probably right. What about us, though? The team. You don't think we're going to split up, do you?"

"I can't lie to you. Things haven't exactly been perfect."

"No, of course not. But we can work things out."

"We can try."

He seemed pleased with this.

"She used to tell me I needed to lose weight."

"Is that why you're eating the little biscuit thing, not the big cake thing?"

"I suppose so. And training. Got to be ready for Sunday."

"We'll be up for it. Don't worry about that."

The wind is behind us in the second half. Before long the game has settled into a period of sullen deadlock. Dan clanks a shot against the post from the edge of the area and we trot back into position without saying a word.

Minutes later we have our best chance of the game. Twisting inside the box, Jerome is hacked down by a green-shirted defender. The ball runs through towards Dan in front of goal, but just as I'm waiting for him to poke it past the goal-keeper something else starts to happen instead.

"Right. That's fucking it."

The Hawk is first on the scene, moving with a litheness not seen at any other stage of the afternoon. With the ball lying abandoned in front of an empty goal the game is transformed into a miniature version of a Western bar brawl as scuffles break out all over the penalty area. Fingers are jabbed into chests, collars are felt and shoulders are bumped. Charlie stomps his foot in the mud and makes a beeline for a ginger-haired midfielder. Before he can get there the vast form of Jamroll rumbles into view and a flat palm sends him backwards.

Now that we're at the shirt-pulling, chest-slapping stage none of us really know what to do next. Even Lars is up out of his goal, waving a fist in the face of the chunky left-winger. In the middle of all this the referee has started peeping his whistle. Whirling left and right he peeps at Keith, then raises a silky arm and peeps at the Hawk as he advances, leering, on two green shirts. Unexpectedly, I recognise the ref as the man in the van this morning eating the huge bag of crisps. It already seems like a very long time ago.

Eventually the panic recedes. We're all a bit tired now. Threatening people can be an exhausting business. I can't help feeling that our chance might have gone in this game. Either that or we've all just chosen to forget what it is we're supposed to be actually doing out here.

There is still time for one last score to be settled. With seconds remaining Lucien scurries forward and is sent sprawling again, this time by Jamroll's slab-like knee.

"Oh Christ. You fucker. Not again."

He looks up from his prone position in the mud as a triangular figure looms above him.

"FACK OFF."

"Oi! Leave him alone."

Like an airship turning in a stiff wind, Jamroll revolves in the direction of Keith's voice. A look of malevolent recognition appears in his small brown eyes.

"Stop kicking people."

"I don't ..."

"Stop. Kicking. People."

"Makes no ..."

"Stop it."

Jamroll isn't built for repartee. There's a pause while he weighs up his options before finally settling on advancing slowly towards Keith. It's like watching a tidal wave about to engulf the Statue of Liberty. Just as he seems on the verge of ingesting Keith into his stomach something stops him in his tracks.

A hand has appeared on the back of Jamroll's neck. His medicine-ball head swivels around. Simon is the same height as him but shaped more like a human being and less like a mountain of old tyres. He stands very tall and very still as he clamps two fingers around Jamroll's cheeks, squashing his lips together like the edges of a giant Cornish pasty.

"Why don't you pick on someone your own size?" he whispers, keeping his arm stretched out in front of him as he marches them both away from Keith.

"What have you got to say for yourself?"

"Faghz...yervoft."

"I can't hear you."

"Fggzzgzz."

"Good. Now why don't we just get on with the game?"

Simon turns and walks away very slowly, leaving a downcast Jamroll completely disarmed. The referee has appeared at his side, circling him like a helicopter buzzing around King Kong. For want of something better to do he restarts play with a dropped ball.

We're not really paying any attention to the game though. Nobody can take their eyes off Simon. Keith is watching him with something close to awe as he takes his position and shrugs his shoulders just to let us know it's still him. Appearances really can be deceptive. For the last twenty years I've just assumed Simon was a skinny, painfully shy tall bloke. Now I know he's a skinny, painfully shy tall bloke who can really put it about when he needs to.

This is the final action of the morning. Moments later the whistle blows and it's all over for another week. We've lost 1–0 but we're calm as we troop back towards the pavilion. I fall into step next to the chunky left-winger and we walk together in silence for a while.

"Sorry about all that back there. We were a bit pumped up today."

"That was nothing." His voice is gently northern.

"Really?"

"We had three players sent off last month. I don't know why. Well, I do. It's Jamroll. He brings it out of people."

"Funny that."

"He's always upset afterwards. He's a lovely lad off the pitch."

Up ahead of us Keith and Jamroll are strolling back towards the clubhouse arm in arm. They're laughing together as Keith reaches up and cuffs the back of his fat neck. And by the time we reach the musty red brick changing room the whole game already seems like a bit of a blur.

It's been a strange morning but not, despite everything, a

bad one. Perhaps a scrappy, breezy Sunday lunchtime isn't too big a deal in the wider scheme of work and family and everything else. We may have failed to win again. We may still be facing extinction. I may be on the verge of a life-changing semi-retirement from the one thing I've done without fail every autumn, winter and spring for the last twenty years. But as I drive home it feels like something malevolent has been left behind on the pitch. And despite the cold, the Sunday traffic, and a feeling that we've all behaved in a way I wouldn't necessarily want anyone else to witness, one thing is clear. I already feel much, much better.

10
Teenage kicks

Only two types of people sit on park benches: old people with nothing else to do and young people with nothing else to do.

"Give me another light. I've gone out."

"That's because you don't inhale."

"Yes I do."

"No you don't. Go on. Watch him."

"Of course I inhale. Dick."

"Dick, yourself."

"Shut up, you lot. Girls at twelve o'clock."

"Where?"

"No. That's six o'clock. I said twelve o'clock. Six more o'clock."

"A bloke with a dog?"

"Oh Christ. Over there. Don't look."

"Oh my God, they're about twelve. You are sick."

Dan lit the stubbly end of my cigarette. Zippo lighters are essential windproof kit both for World War Two fighter pilots and for sixteen-year-old boys on their way home from school.

"You're right. They are about twelve," Simon sighed. In his

hand, only slightly concealed, he was holding a plastic bottle of strong cider. It was Friday afternoon and, technically, this was the second half of our games lesson. It had become such a routine with us now that we didn't even have to say anything. Friday 1.15 was home time.

"What's in the bag?"

"I went down to Bass Box."

Dan took a record out of Simon's carrier bag and held it up in front of him.

"Give it back."

" 'Big Beats' by Big Feet featuring Chantelle. Sounds wicked."

"It's intelligent drum and bass. Their old stuff was more jump up and breakbeat."

"You know what this is?"

"What?"

"It's a cry for help. Maybe there's someone at school you could talk to. Give me that bottle."

"Mallory coach."

"Where?"

"Over there."

The Mallory coach ran to and from the local girls' school. It passed by this way every Friday afternoon. The road was just close enough to give a glimpse of blue blazer, long hair and maybe the back of a head. We watched as the coach disappeared down to the turn in the road by the Horse and Jockey.

"Why don't girls pull moonies?" Simon wondered aloud. "If I was a girl I'd moony all the time. It would be about the only thing I ever did."

"Did you see them checking me out?" Dan said.

"Wondering who that bloke with the orange hair is, you mean?"

In the last six months Dan and I had been through some self-destructive experiments with black hair dye. We'd learned a lot from the experience. For a start we'd learned that you're not allowed to go to school with dyed black hair. We'd also learned that the only way of getting it out is bleaching your hair so it goes first orange and then finally a dull green. It has to be said we were our own harshest critics. Even now I still shudder if I find even the smallest tinge of ginger in my sideburns.

"What's going on tonight?" Dan asked.

"There's two parties. One at Jessie's house and then your thing."

"Those girls in my street. It's more of a gathering. They've got a free house."

"Let's meet here, get some beers, go to the party."

"I can't," Simon said.

"What's your problem?"

"My parents want me to stay in."

"Don't be gayer than you already are."

"If they told you to jump off a cliff, would you do it?"

"No. I'd put my hand in a fire."

"There'll be loads of fit girls there."

"And desperate twelve-year-olds."

"My parents are already hassling me about it. And I want to go to the game tomorrow."

"I saw Terry today. His brother's got the tickets. His mates are going to be there. They said it might get nasty."

"Wicked."

"Wicked."

Football always has been a rough game. It's just the way it turned out and the way it carried on. The first proper matches were Shrovetide games in Derbyshire, huge free-for-alls with half the parish joining in the general drunken throng, a chance to run around like a maniac and settle old scores with the next village along. The games were eventually outlawed. In the end the army were sent in to break it up.

This kind of thing has always been a part of football's appeal. Particularly when you're sixteen years old. Dan and I may have bunked off games every week but we still played. Where else do you get to spend an hour and a half kicking, pushing and tripping a group of complete strangers and then walk away with a handshake at the end of it all?

School was different. If you've never found school boring then you've probably never been to school. My record had always been patchy. I was good at some things and really bad at others. But at least I was reliable. I always failed the same subjects. Not that this made life any easier for my teachers.

School may have been out, but football was definitely still in. Bexley Warriors were different from other teams I'd been in. These were difficult times for football and me. Something had been lost along the way. I knew I wasn't going to be a footballer. None of us were. For now all I really wanted to do was get up late, run about a bit and spend the rest of the time either sleeping or mucking about with my friends. At Bexley you could do all of this.

Dan and I had been playing for Bexley for almost a year and it suited us down to the ground. We played on AstroTurf on Saturday afternoons. Our coach was a quiet, bearded man called Steve, who pretty much let us get on with things. I think he just liked having something to do at the weekends.

"Do be careful. And make sure you eat something while you're out," my mum used to say as I passed her in the kitchen on a Saturday, my boots inside my canvas bag.

"Yeah-eah."

"Are you going out with Dan and Steven?"

"Simon." My mum always liked Dan. Mothers do for some reason.

"When will you be back?"

"Next week some time. Definitely by April."

"Okay. Be careful on that bike."

We'd moved house from Brockley to Lewisham. This was where my friends from school all lived, as well as the girls we'd got to know from Mallory. People's homes had become places you tramped through on your way up to the sanctuary of the bedroom. Dan's place was best. He had a loft room at the top of the house with a door you could lock and a window you could climb out of on to the roof.

My brother had left school the year before and gone to college in Brighton. He came back for the holidays but even then he was hardly around. Life could have been boring if it wasn't for all the other stuff taking me out of the house these days, like fags and cans of weak lager from the Turkish off-licence and going round to people's houses and, looking back, more regularly than any of these, playing football.

Now there was something else too: watching football. I'd been taken to see most of the local teams when I was a little kid. I'd been to Charlton with George and Crystal Palace with my cousins. I'd followed England on the TV. But none of this had made much impression. For a sixteen-year-old boy in south-east London there was only one real option. A single name rumbled in the background of every kickabout, every Saturday afternoon shopping trip, and every bunch of casuals barging down the train from Charing Cross to New Cross. It had to be Millwall.

Dan and I had started going with some of the kids from Bexley Warriors. Terry could get tickets. Terry's brother had a friend of a friend who worked at the club. He was our man. Unfortunately Terry's brother also brought something else with him, namely himself and his mates.

Terry's brother's mates were the kind of people you had to pretend you weren't scared of. We managed to avoid them most of the time. Not that we'd have admitted we were doing it. In principle you wanted to be seen around with Terry's brother's mates. You wanted to be able to drop their names in conversation. But only in principle.

We walked down from the heath towards Dan's house, Simon with his plastic bag of records, me with my canvas satchel. Simon was already tall and much skinnier than he is now. His school uniform ended in the wrong places, above his ankles and short of his wrists, but still had plenty to give in the neck and the shoulders.

"Terry said the tickets are a tenner. He got them from his brother. We're behind the goal."

"Wicked."

"Get there for two he said."

We walked on in silence.

"Is Kevin Coles going?" Dan asked casually.

"I don't know. Probably."

Everybody knew about Kevin Coles. He'd been stabbed once with a kitchen knife. He carried a metal chain. He stole motorbikes. He'd been arrested for fighting more times than you could count. I'd seen him around. He was short and nondescript, a couple of years older than us, but with a razor-blade smile that even from a distance made your skin creep slightly.

"What about tonight then?" Simon said.

"What about it?"

"Who's going to be there? Is Natalie around?"

"Probably. You're not going though."

"I just wondered."

"You fancy her, don't you?"

"No."

"She told me she really liked you. She said, who's that lanky freak you hang around with? I really like him. A lot."

"Shut your face."

"Why don't you play her some intelligent drum and bass. She'll go wild for it."

"If you don't shut up I'll tell Kevin Coles you pulled his sister."

"As if I did though."

"He's going to stab you up."

"With a kitchen knife."

"Kevin's my mate actually."

We were at Dan's door now. He let himself in with his key.

"Come round later."

"All right."

"Maybe."

"Dick."

I walked home quickly, thinking about whether my breath smelt of fags, whether to tell Simon that me and Dan had both snogged Natalie at her friend's house the weekend before and, mainly, about why we couldn't go to the football without getting mixed up with Terry, Terry's brother and Terry's brother's mates. It always seemed to happen that way. But then going to Millwall had never been simple.

The first time I went to watch them play was with George and his older brother. On the last stretch of the walk to the stadium, I could feel the hairs start to stand up on the back of my neck. Men covered in large tattoos – in the days when tattoos were a sign of being hard, rather than a sign of being a student – spilt out of dingy brown boozers. There were police on horseback but even they seemed to hang back from the crowds.

Inside the ground we were installed on a crowded terrace with a terrible view of the pitch and immediately abandoned by the elder brother so that he could go and hang out with some other kids with wedge haircuts, white trainers and Lacoste tennis shirts.

George and I barely said a word for the full ninety minutes. We spent the game listening to the people around us. Football didn't seem to be that important here. What mattered was shouting and swearing as much as possible. The noise would gather like a roll of thunder at the far side of the ground. Suddenly a swell at one end would rumble towards us like a furious Mexican wave. Now this was something. I wasn't sure it was football, but it was certainly something. I'd been going back ever since.

Over the years there was football at the Den too. I saw a young John Fashanu, fantastically strong and aggressive. I saw Teddy Sheringham sent off for stamping on someone's head and I followed his goal-scoring partnership with Tony Cascarino. I admired fearsome bubble-permed hardman Terry Hurlock and his midfield henchman Les Briley, part of a First Division team that held Manchester United to a 0–0 draw at a packed and shuddering Den.

There was menace in the air in those days. Millwall have got a new chairman now and a new stadium and a different approach to things. Back then Bermondsey on a Saturday afternoon was a pretty scary place. It's a strange part of London. It can feel remote and cut off from the rest of the city. At times it felt like there wasn't much there really, just concrete and scraggy trees and, in the middle of it all, a football ground.

The next day was mild and breezy. The morning seemed to drag. Usually I'd be playing for Bexley on a Saturday. I had to remind myself not to bother with my usual routine, packing my bag first thing and eating a bowl of cereal for lunch while

I watched *Grandstand*. Instead I kicked around in my room, dressed and ready to go in my best trainers and baggy jeans.

I called round for Simon and we picked up Dan and headed up to the bus stop. Traffic lights turned to green as we chugged down the hill and the roads were almost empty as we sped through Deptford and then along the wide, ragged streets of New Cross.

"How was last night?" Simon asked.

"It was all right."

The party had been just like parties always were: most of it spent loitering with your mates, followed by a confused period of social interaction sparked by some brave soul, and all ended prematurely by the return around midnight of the grinning parents.

"Did you pull?"

"Actually, yes. I did. Some girl called Becky."

In fact Dan had been discovered in a small laundry room, only emerging as the lights were being turned on and bottles gathered up in plastic rubbish bags.

"I'm on a roll. That's three in three weeks."

"Fluke."

"There's no such thing as fluke. You make your own luck."

Back then snogging girls was a bit like being a centre forward playing week in week out. You're always aware of your scoring ratio. You know when the last one was and you're always thinking about the next. Sometimes you get on a golden run where everything you try seems to come off. It's a confidence thing.

Occasionally there are droughts too. Every teenage boy has been through the tough times where you just need that little bit of luck, plus maybe half a bottle of Kahlua. The same rules apply though. You're only ever as good as your last pull. Right now Dan was in mid-season form. Everything was falling for him.

It was a short walk up the hill from the bus stop to the little park where we'd arranged to meet Terry and the boys. We didn't say much on the way. It didn't seem like a strange place to be meeting. We were used to parks and recs and heaths.

"Did anyone tell Steve we weren't coming to football?"

"I said last week."

"Did he get someone else?"

"I don't know. What do you care anyway?"

The park was empty apart from a couple of kids on the swings. Terry and the boys were huddled around a bench in the far corner.

"All right, lads," Terry said, looking small and furtive in a blue tracksuit top. "You know Joey, don't you?"

Terry's brother looked up, nodded and then went back to talking to the large, square, flat-nosed bloke next to him.

"This is Vinnie and Kevin."

Kevin Coles was small, dark and menacingly still. Vinnie looked across without showing any signs of actually being able to see us. We stood around while he talked for a long time about a VW Beetle he'd been dismantling.

"Stoke today," Joey said, shaking his head. "Fucking Stoke."

"Stoke," we agreed.

"What about Stoke?" I asked.

"What about Stoke? Stoke are well hard. Stoke are nutters."

Vinnie's expression suggested there must be something quite seriously wrong with me if I didn't know Stoke were nutters.

"Last year it kicked right off. There'll be police all over the place today."

Next to me Simon had gone very pale. In his green bomber jacket, limp like an old lettuce leaf, he looked even thinner than normal. Vinnie had produced something from his pocket.

"Anyone got a light?"

Dan held out his Zippo. I watched as Vinnie lit a large, white, crumpled roll-up. I'd been at parties where people smoked dope, but never in a park, at lunchtime, with the sun breaking through the cobbled grey and white clouds. The joint was passed to Vinnie's left. Joey was next to him. Two more and it would be me. It looked huge and snub-nosed, laden like a nuclear warhead.

The tip glowed as Simon, who didn't smoke and who caught colds and used to bring an inhaler to football, drew deeply. Watery-eyed, he handed it straight to me. Just like a cigarette, I told myself, puffing twice and feeling a burn at the back of my throat. Fortunately Joey and Vinnie had started talking about paying for the tickets. I managed to get rid of it after a respectable amount of time without actually raising it to my mouth again.

"Cheers."

"Is your mate all right? Oi, tall boy. Fucking hell, look at the size of him. If it goes off I'm getting behind you."

Simon half opened his mouth to say something and then closed it again.

"What's up with you, big lad? You ready for a ruck?"

"Simon's always up for it," Dan said from behind me. "I wouldn't mess with him."

"Yeah?"

"He just flips," Dan clicked his fingers, "like that. Famous for it."

By now Simon had wandered off to tie his shoelace on a bench.

"I'll take your word for it." Vinnie pocketed a crumpled roll of tenners. "Right, we'd better get down there."

We walked in step along the wide pavement until we got to the main road. Dodging past buses and a solid line of cars turning right towards the ground, we found ourselves sucked up into a stream of people all heading the same way. The crowd thickened around us as we shuffled past newsagents, an off-licence with grilles across the windows and a kebab shop with a queue stretching out of the door and down the road. In front of us a man in a nylon coat was smoking a cigar. The smell made me feel sick; up ahead we saw the mounted police for the first time.

"Pigs," Joey said twitchily. From behind us a chant began to ripple though the crowd and suddenly we were singing too as beyond the police line we caught sight of the massed red and white of Stoke.

"Miw-waw, Mi-iw-waw, Miw-waw, Miw-waw, Miw-waw, Mi-iw-waw, Miw-*waw*!"

Our seats were right behind the goal. The pitch rolled away from us, a gaudy green rectangle. At the far end a mass of red and white was packed into a tight little corner of seating. There was no way of standing still. You just had to move with the swell of the crowd. We were squeezed so tight I could feel breath on my neck.

"Yeh-er-wankah!" Terry's brother shouted as the Stoke keeper jogged across to the goalmouth in front of us. Immediately a huge and booming voice took up the cry from behind.

"Hyourgurna-ged-yor-fughinedgickedin!"

The voice from behind echoed like a bass woofer deep in my chest. I glanced across at Simon. He was standing half crouched, bending away from it like a reed in the wind. Chancing a look, I caught sight of the voice's owner. He was huge, a vast collage of shaved head, bristly jaw and deep-set, dark-rimmed eyes that seemed flat in his head rather than round. He took up the space of three men. Even Vinnie looked narrow-shouldered and fragile next to him.

To huge indignation the game kicked off, and for the next forty-five minutes the back of my neck was blistered by the bellowing voice. It rumbled across the heads like a sudden clap of thunder. In glimpses I managed to remind myself that Vinnie and, best of all, Kevin Coles were still there. Except, something really bad had started to happen. Joey had started talking to the group behind us.

"Come on, you fucking wankers," a voice shouted.

"Oi, you want some, do you?"

"What's he doing?" I whispered.

"I have no idea."

"Why is he talking to those lunatics?"

Simon looked moon-faced and slightly ill. "Maybe because if anything goes wrong I can just flip. I'm famous for it."

Half-time arrived in a blur. We stood very still, hoping this might make us invisible. Just as the voice finished a lengthy bellowing at the red-and-white fans in the distance, I made the mistake of looking round. The flat eyeballs swivelled in my direction. I stared back, unable to stop myself from smiling feebly.

"Jesus Christ. What the fuck have we got here?"

This seemed relatively friendly. I could handle this. The huge face loomed closer.

"Pretty boys. A bunch of fucking pretty boys."

I managed to nod and shake my head at the same time.

"Lovely fucking boys." Reaching out a slab-like hand he grabbed Dan around the neck and cradled him in the crook of his arm. There was a burst of growled laughter and then mercifully Dan was back on his feet and the bull neck was being flexed in another direction as something else caught its attention.

"What. The. Fuck," Dan muttered.

"You're a pretty boy," Simon said.

"It isn't funny. He's a big, bald, mad queer."

"Just stick with Terry and the others. We'll be okay with them."

What *was* Kevin doing now? He still looked seriously unbothered by being here. Things would be fine. Just as long as we stuck with him. Kevin was our ace in the hole.

As the second half kicked off the invisible screen separating us from the people behind seemed to have been raised. Joey was shoved to the ground in a bundle of arms and legs. He laughed painfully as he got to his feet. A can of lager thrown from behind splattered Vinnie's jacket collar. He didn't look back.

"Come on, lads! Fucking sing! Fucking louder!"

Weepily we mouthed along with the words. I tried to make myself shrink into the ground as a knee crunched into my back and, after a near miss in the far goal, a hand slapped me hard across the side of my head, leaving my ear humming. With a few minutes left of the longest half of football I'd ever seen, something really terrible happened. We scored.

There was bedlam. Bodies tumbled and writhed. A huge, gnarled man was hurled forward, landing three rows in front of us. For a second I lost sight of daylight. When I resurfaced I was being embraced by the massive skinhead with the booming voice. His sandpaper face scraped my cheek. A deep and lingering yell rumbled in my left ear. Freed by a sudden mass chant towards the Stoke fans, I struggled up off the floor.

Moments later the final whistle blew. Turning to sneak away, we found ourselves enveloped by the group behind us. "Something's going down," a voice said. There were discussions. I saw Joey nodding, Vinnie handing out cigarettes, and suddenly we were being carried away with the crowd towards the exit.

"What's happening?" Simon whispered.

"I don't know. Something's going down."

"What do we do?"

"Follow Kevin."

The crush of bodies swept us down the stairs and out of the ground. There was no room to turn and flee. In front of me I could see a wall of shoulders and thick necks. Up ahead in the distance there was a line of police on horseback in riot gear and beyond them the red and white of Stoke. The noise level had begun to rise. I tried to back away but kicks from behind kept us going forward. Suddenly there was space to run. Kevin appeared next to us, looking wide-eyed and ready for action.

"Stay close to me," he said quietly. "Do what I do."

We followed at a jog as the police line loomed closer. Someone threw something. A horse reared up, its eyes white behind the plastic shield. I felt like I was floating forward, out of control. My movements were controlled entirely by the noise of the running feet behind me.

"Now!"

Kevin tugged at my shoulder and suddenly we were scuttling sideways, all six of us hurtling down a flight of steps and into a housing estate.

"Just run."

Moving fast, we cut back away from the ground and up the hill towards the park where we'd met that afternoon. I could hear laughter around me as a weird kind of giggle rose in my own throat. Finally we stopped, doubled up against a sleepy-looking tree. The park was still empty. There was no sound of running feet behind us. It took a while to find my voice.

"What happened back there?"

Kevin was still breathing hard between his sharp little teeth.

"How do you mean?"

"It's just, I thought you were up for all that."

"Are you kidding? Did you see those blokes?"

"What about you though? You know. The chain. The bread knife."

"What bread knife?

"You were stabbed with a bread knife."

There was a pause. "That's a really horrible thing to say."

"Sorry."

We walked home the long way. Dan and Simon both looked completely zonked. Dan's hair was sticking up. His eyes were drooping and red-rimmed.

"How come you're okay?" he said after a while.

"How do you mean?"

"That spliff totally knocked me out," Simon said.

"Exactly."

"I've got ways of dealing with it."

"What does that mean?"

"I don't inhale, remember."

"You dick."

"Did you see me? I was right in there."

"Right in there crapping your pants."

We never did go to a game with Terry again. Things have changed a lot since then. Dan and I don't go to watch Millwall very much these days. Following a team was more of a teenage thing for me. It's not such a frightening place any more, and maybe not such an exciting one either. We're older, too, of course. I'm not sure I'd give up playing football to go and watch a game, like we did when we were sixteen.

In fact I know I wouldn't. Watching football comes in and out of fashion but playing doesn't ever change. You do it because you want to. There's nothing else to it. It's a friendly kind of place too, once you step out of the changing rooms and over the white line. Anybody can do it and everybody's welcome. The playing field, unless you're on the top pitch at Halfmarshes with its gentle slope down towards the far end, is always even.

11
Home

Sunday February 6th 2005
Bolingbroke Athletic vs.
Colorama Print and Design Services Ltd

Speed is a mysterious thing. It's not a product of muscle build or hours in the gym. Real speed comes from rhythm rather than power. People who can really run often look like they're not trying at all. I used to play with a left-winger who could do the hundred metres in eleven seconds. I can remember watching him glide away and thinking how unfair it was that so little effort could produce so much power.

I once heard Trevor Brooking talk about trying to increase his speed as a player. He was advised to take shorter strides and to bend forward from the hips as he started off. I decided to try this the next time I played. At first I kept forgetting. When I did remember I looked like a drunk running for the last night bus. I've got a low-stepping style. My head rocks from side to side. Over ten yards, I'm slow. Over thirty yards I'm slightly less slow. And over fifty yards I've stopped.

Why am I telling you all this? Because sometimes you just have to be quick. And from where we're standing, it still looks like Keith might make it to the safety of the changing rooms.

"Keep left. No, don't get stuck round the cricket pitch."

By now Keith is a white speck in the distance. Behind him two figures are closing in. The nearest one, Kirsty, is wearing a pink jacket and has bouncing curly hair. A few metres behind, Sam is making a detour to the left to cut off Keith's flank. A slighter figure with matching hat and boots, she's got a golf umbrella in one hand. It looks like they're all still talking, although to be honest Keith doesn't seem to be getting much of a look-in.

"They never should have banned hunting," Dave says. "I can see why people are into it now."

"You can still hunt if you want to. There's a bunch of kids on Shepherd's Bush Green every Saturday night on bikes with pit-bulls. They ride along behind while the dogs chase the rats and the pigeons. That's hunting."

"Look. They've nearly got him to stand still."

"Probably the last we'll ever see of him."

"My money's on Kirsty with the umbrella in the car park."

How did this happen? As usual it all began with the best of intentions. As usual it was all Keith's idea. And as always seems to be the case these days, it started off as a way of helping us actually win a game of football.

"We need more support," Keith had announced, shaking out his towel. "We're at home next week. We need to get a proper crowd in."

"Who are we going to persuade to come and watch us?"

"There's loads of people. Everybody's got someone. Girlfriends, wives, parents. We've got to do something. We can't go on like this."

We'd just lost 3–1 to a team of policemen. They were tough, competitive and surprisingly dirty. At least they apologised after they'd kicked you. At the final whistle a man with a head like a skull shook my hand so fiercely I could almost hear the bones in my fingers grating together. The police turned out to have superior changing rooms and really good showers. We'd all lingered a bit longer than normal to make the most of it.

"Are you going to bring Bobby?" I asked Dan.

"You must be joking."

"I thought she was around next week."

"Oh. Yeah. Well, she might be."

"I'll bring Kate if we can dump the kids," Dave said. "And if she'll come."

"As long as Jerome brings that Kelly," Nev said thoughtfully.

That Kelly is Jerome's girlfriend. She came to our drinks at Christmas. She's not much more than twenty and she's a dancer. She talked to Nev for at least half an hour in the pub, although that was before she managed to get a table, a whole set of chairs and a fruit machine between the two of them.

"You're a sick man."

"Why? What's wrong with admiring someone's girlfriend?"

"Admiring is fine. You're not supposed to talk about it."

"What's the difference?"

"It's how you do it," Dan says. "I can tell Lucien I think Pru's a pretty girl. It doesn't mean I fancy her."

"Why not? What's wrong with her?"

"There's nothing wrong. If you must know I think she's very fit."

"Oi. That's my missus you're talking about."

"Exactly. You can't win."

"The point is we need all the help we can get," Keith said, zipping up the kit bag. "So let's just try and get someone down to support us. We're doing this to stay alive, remember."

On Monday Laura was in a good mood when she got home from work. I found her sitting on the sofa with a glass of wine in her hand. This seemed like as good a time as any.

"Something weird happened to me on the Tube," she said, not taking her eyes off an advert on the TV for leather futons. "This man offered me his seat."

"What's weird about that?"

"I didn't want to sit down, so I gave it to this old guy. Then the first bloke tried to take it back."

"He can't do that. It's your seat."

"That's just it, though. He said he gave it to me, not this other bloke."

"So what happened?"

"The older guy started trying to make his wife sit in it."

"Guilt treatment. Did it work?"

"Not really. It was pretty obvious he wanted to sit in it himself."

"So who got the seat?"

"We found this really old man at the other end of the carriage and made him take it."

"Nice move. None of you get the seat, but no one gets to complain. Listen, what are you doing this weekend?"

"I might go and see Abigail. Why? Are you asking me out?"

"There was something."

"Let's do it. Where shall we go? How about Edinburgh? I know we talked about it, but, you know, something always gets in the way ..."

"The thing is ... do you want to come to watch us on Sunday? Keith thought if we had some support, it might help."

"You want me to watch you play football?"

"Yeah. I'm sorry. I'd really like to go away as well but ..."

"I know. You don't have to tell me."

She took her glass and went into the bedroom. I sat there trying to think of something to say while she fiddled with the pots she keeps in the window box. Outside it was raining. Nothing unusual, just an everyday drizzle. I've never been good at talking people around. It must be nice to be able to charm your way out of a tight corner. Where do they get it from, these people with charm? Either way it didn't look like Laura would be coming to football. Maybe this wasn't entirely a bad thing.

Against all odds, as the week wore on an unexpected momentum began to build. Lars would be bringing his wife, Yana. Keith was coming with whoever his current on-off girl-friend was. Simon had even persuaded his sister Sally to make an appearance. It looked like if we were going down, at least we were going to do it in front of our loved ones and close family members. Despite this, not everybody was looking forward to it as much as they might have been.

Jerome called me on Wednesday, just as I was writing a list of the top fifty footballers with unusual beards and/or mous-taches. We work near each other, so we have lunch sometimes.

The restaurant where he works serves lobster and steak to people from the City who want to impress either their clients or their secretary. It's just a shame we always go next door to the café with plastic tables where the owner shouts your order through a hatch and it appears, as if by magic, a few moments later.

"Bacon! Chips! Egg!"

"Why can't we eat at your place for a change?"

"Two toast! Sausage! Bake bean!"

"Because I like going out. Anyway we get our potatoes from the same place."

"You don't deep-fry everything."

"No. We sauté."

"What about my five portions of fruit and vegetables?"

"Vegetables are overrated. When did you ever see a tiger eating celery?"

"Dinosaurs ate rocks."

"Exactly."

"They're extinct."

"Now they are. But before that."

Two huge plates of food appeared in front of us. Jerome started at one side and gradually worked his way across to the other.

"So what's up?" I asked.

He finished a mouthful. "Oh yeah. Football on Sunday. I wanted to have a word with you about it."

"Why me?"

"Why not you? You're the best man for the job."

I had a moment of déjà vu. Hadn't I already been here with

Nev and the mysterious disappearance of Mrs Nev? Personally, I'd never confide in me. People always do for some reason. I think it's my face. But then few things can be as misleading as the way someone's face looks.

"The thing is, don't you think Keith goes on a bit about the team? Maybe it isn't such a big deal. Sometimes I look around and think I'd be better off out of it."

"You're younger than us. It's different for you. You can stop and it doesn't mean giving up for good."

"Only four years."

"It's a big difference. Things catch up with you."

"Anyway, if I ask Kelly she'll come, but I'm not sure I want to. At the moment if I see her on Saturday night, Sunday's for me. I don't want to get serious."

"You don't know when you've got it easy."

"What's that supposed to mean?"

"You're still young, there's so much you have to go through. Find a girl, settle down, if you want you can marry her. Look at me, I am old but I'm happy."

"You don't look that happy."

"Never mind. What do you think she's going to do? See you playing football and decide you've got to get married immediately? Take it from me. It's not likely."

It really hadn't seemed like such a big deal at the time. Bring someone down, Keith said. And why not? When I got home that night Laura was cooking dinner.

"What time are we going on Sunday?" she said, tasting something on a spoon.

"10.30 start. If you fancy it."

"Only if you still want me to come."

"Of course I do."

"I talked to Bobby earlier. We're going to take a packed lunch with us. And blankets. I'm quite looking forward to it."

Sunday morning was cold and bright. Maybe it was just me, but for some reason I found it quite hard to get to sleep the night before. At a final count there were fifteen wives, girl-friends, family members and flatmates, as well as Keith's mum, all coming down to watch us take on a Colorama Print and Design Services XI at a muddy and desolate Fishponds.

"It's a lovely day," Laura said as we turned into the car park. The frost lingered in the shadows like snow, and from a distance the pitch was completely white. She was wearing gloves, a scarf and her furry hat. In the boot she'd packed what looked like a small suitcase.

"Where are the changing rooms?"

"You're looking at them."

"That little hut?"

"Yes. That little hut."

Outside we lined up sheepishly, like people being forced to mix at a party. I hadn't really thought about how this was going to feel. I don't think any of us had. Pretty awful, turned out to be the answer to that one. I introduced Laura to Bob and Mrs Bob. There's not much to choose between the two of them.

"Don't worry about the cold. I've got a little something in here to keep us going," she said, pointing to her handbag.

Pru and Lucien were both in black. Pru is one of those

cheerful Goths. She smiles a lot and her hair is really more red than black. It's like she's making a covert escape bid. Dave was there with Kate and Jamie, one of the kids. Simon and his sister Sally were standing in the doorway, both of them ridiculously tall. Jerome and Kelly were talking to Laura. He caught my eye and shrugged. A girl with curly hair, wearing a tightly zipped pink jacket, was standing next to Keith. Simon mouthed something at me over her shoulder.

"Kirsty," I said, getting it. "This is Laura."

"Hello."

"Hello, boys. Hello, Dan, love."

Maureen, Keith's mum, knows all of us. She's even been to our team dinners in the past. Sometimes I get the impression she still thinks we're all twelve years old. Standing next to Dan she gave Bobby the once-over. Bobby was wearing sunglasses, a white scarf and surely way too few items of clothing for a freezing Sunday in Tooting.

The opposition had arrived by now. They hovered in the background, not sure what to make of the crowd. In the distance a new four-wheel-drive car had pulled up. A bulky figure struggled upright under the weight of a huge sports bag. A few yards in front, Nev's wife waited patiently. Her hair was a bright shade of artificial blonde and even from a distance her suntan was impressive.

"Lads. Ladies. Mum," Keith shouted out. "If you can wait here a moment, we've got to get changed now. Kick-off in twenty minutes. Thank you."

In the changing room we were unusually quiet. The normal

pre-match butterflies had completely failed to kick in. Instead, I just felt really tired. Only Charlie seemed unaffected, whistling between his teeth as he taped up his socks. Keith went to the door and peered outside. The noise level rose. Bobby said something and there were murmurs of agreement and some laughter. He closed it again.

"Lads, let's get switched on," he said, turning to face us. "This is a game we can win. We've got the support we wanted ..."

"Christ knows what we've got," Dan said.

"Listen, we wanted this and now we've got it. Let's just go out there and put on a show. And do me a favour. If Sam turns up, my ex, don't let her talk to Kirsty."

"Which one's Sam?"

"Small. Brunette. I thought I'd asked her to come down today. Then first thing this morning Kirsty's outside ringing on the doorbell."

Colorama were already on the pitch as we jogged across towards the rows of scarves and hats on the touchline. In front of me, Nev seemed to be muttering to himself. As we got closer I stopped to talk to Kate, Dave's wife. We've always got on well. She's one of the calmest people I know, even when she's got three kids hanging off her arm. Usually I'd probably be a bit intimidated by her. I don't know why I'm not.

"Are you cold?"

"No, I'm fine. I'll be running around in a bit."

She laughed. "Actually I was talking to Jamie. But I'm glad you're all right too."

"Oi. Get over here," Keith shouted from the middle of the pitch.

"Sorry. Better go."

"Jesus, look at him," Dan said as I joined the huddle. "Happy now?"

"What do you mean?"

"Oh my God. He doesn't fancy Mrs Dave?"

"Of course I don't."

"You're a sick man. She's got kids," Jerome said, shaking his head.

We kicked a few practice balls around on the edge of the penalty area, gathered as far away from our own supporters as possible.

"Come on, boys," Mrs Nev shouted. There was more laughter. Next to me Lucien looked pale, even paler than usual. In the goalmouth Lars stood with his hands in his pockets. Casting a final anxious glance across towards the changing rooms, Keith called us together again.

"Lads, let's get straight on with this. I know it feels a bit weird. But we need to put in a performance today. We can beat these."

"It's not weird. It just isn't natural."

"Whose stupid idea was this anyway?"

As Colorama kicked off there were a few shouts, but none from us. Nobody said much at all. Nobody swore. Nobody even complained when Jerome picked up possession, jinked forward on the right and then just stopped. At one point Nev actually ran away from the ball. On the touchline a circle had gathered around his wife, who seemed to be telling a long story.

Listlessly, the game meandered from box to box. Lars scuffed a goal kick straight out of play and we watched in silence as it bounced down towards the railway. Moments later Dan was hacked down by a curly-haired midfielder who looked about seventeen years old. As he sprang back up to his feet, ready for a fight, there was a groan of disapproval from behind us.

"He's sweet. Look at his hair."

"His little knees."

The curly-haired midfielder winked as he ran past the referee. This really wasn't going very well at all. One thing about football, however: there's always scope for things to get worse. Before long we were 1–0 down. A long free kick was swung in from the right and deflected past Lars, unchallenged, from inside the six-yard box. At least nobody seemed to notice on the touchline. Bob's wife was passing around plastic cups. I saw Laura wince as she took a sip. Next to her Bobby was wrapped from head to toe in a blanket, just her sunglasses visible beneath a fur-rimmed hood.

Soon it was 2–0. With Nev still staring towards the crowd, a long pass bobbled through where he might have been standing. A tall, skinny-legged number nine picked up the ball and galloped off towards goal. Bearing down on Lars, he scuffed a shot slowly into the corner of the net. There was a shriek from somewhere. The grey shirts converged in celebration and we trooped upfield for the restart.

"Shit," Keith muttered.

"It's only 2–0."

"Not that. She's here. See over there? That's Sam."

A skinny girl with fiercely tied-back hair was standing next to Keith's mum and seeming to stare very hard at pink-jacketed Kirsty. For the rest of the half Keith didn't run very much. In fact when the whistle blew for the break it took a while for any of us to move.

"Shall we go off then?" Bob suggested at last.

"I think we'd better."

"It might look weird."

We gathered on the touchline. Next to me Janet wiped some mud off Nev's face with a paper handkerchief. Bob's wife handed him his coat and scarf.

"Margaret, I'm fine."

"You'll catch your death."

Laura looked happy enough.

"So what do you do now?" she asked.

"Have a rest."

"Out here in the cold?"

"Yes."

"Nothing to eat or drink?"

"We did have some energy drinks once."

She shook her head. "It's not much of a break. Who's that girl by the way?"

Sam was talking very quickly to Keith, who was nodding sympathetically, all the while trying to back away very slowly.

"She said something about Kirsty."

"Kirsty said something about her," Sally added.

"It's Keith stuff. Best to stay out. Laura, you know Dave and Kate."

At least Dave seemed relaxed. We shared a plastic cup of tea. He was wearing little Jamie's woolly hat and helping her peel a banana while she kicked him repeatedly in the shins. At another time I might have been thinking thank God that's not me. Not today though. For one thing, he actually looked quite happy.

"Er, lads. Sorry. Sorry, ladies," Keith called out, eventually managing to gather enough of us off to one side for a half-time talk.

"Right. Two–nil down against this lot. It's a fucking joke. Second half I want you in hard and first to the ball ..."

"Speak up."

Keith waved a hand. "Just give us a second," he shouted. "Bob and Si, I want you pushing up from the front. Work the channels, come short and go long."

"Tea anyone?"

"When can we go home? The men are being boring."

"Do you like McDonald's?" Dan said. He was standing next to little Jamie. She looked up at him with wide eyes.

"I bet you do."

"Actually we don't encourage Jamie to ..."

"Daddy, I want to go to McDonald's."

"There's one in the shopping centre. Just over there," Dan said.

"Shopping centre?"

"Let's go. I need coffee," Bobby said from deep inside her hood.

"I need heat."

"I need the loo."

Bags were packed and coats buttoned. Moments later our group of supporters were heading across the field in the direction of Tooting High Street, where they would eventually find a Lithuanian internet café, three kebab houses and lots of shops selling nothing but soap powder and kitchen roll. Sometimes Dan can be a genius.

"Right," Keith said, turning back to us.

"This was all your idea."

"Get some support down he says."

"All right, all right. I'm in more trouble than any of you here. Forget all that lot. Let's just get back out there and give it some."

Unexpectedly, this was exactly what we did. From the start we steamed forward like dogs let off the leash. Seconds into the half Dan played a neat pass through to Lucien, who skipped past his defender and curled a shot just wide.

"Come on, whites!"

"More of that!"

We were a different team now. All over the pitch white shirts snapped into tackles. Before long the curly-haired midfielder had been sent flying by a two-footed lunge, then crashing into the mud after a shoulder barge that left Keith with the ball at his feet.

"Tackle, whites."

"Play on."

We kept coming forward. Jerome beat two players and scuffed his shot wide of goal. Twice the ball clanked back off a post. Suddenly the Colorama players were like passers-by caught up in somebody else's game. And eventually we did score, Dan poking in a bouncing shot that found the far corner of the net.

We sprinted back for the restart, hungry for more. Still there was no let-up. Lars cleared the ball huge distances, Simon leapt and harried, Charlie slid in for tackles. And for the first time this season, the first time I could remember in fact, it felt as though we were in total control of the game. Surely this time it had to come.

"Oh, they're going the other way, are they?" a voice said from the touchline.

"Yes, I think they are," someone else agreed.

I suppose some things just aren't meant to be. Unobserved, the convoy of familiar faces had reoccupied the near touchline. By the halfway line Nev scuffed the ball straight out of play for a throw-in as, nearby, shopping bags were placed in a pile. Mrs Bob studied the side of a box of soap powder. Close to me Kirsty and Sam were standing next to each other. At least they were talking now. Although they still didn't look that happy.

The time seemed to have flown by. Somehow there were only five minutes to go now as Keith shanked a pass straight to a grey shirt. Dan missed a tackle. Dave was caught looking the wrong way completely. And that was it for us. As quickly as it had appeared, our momentum seemed to evaporate. We shuffled through the final moments, desperate suddenly for an end to it all. The final whistle blew just as Keith slid in for a tackle. Even from my side of the pitch his ankle made a twanging sound as it turned in the turf.

"Are you all right, Keith?"

A huddle had already formed around him on the touchline.

"Oh shit, shit, shit," he said, rolling down his sock. "Kirsty, love, can you get me some ice? From the box over there. Oh shit."

"Get it yourself."

"Go on. Just some ice."

"Why don't you ask your girlfriend?"

"What's that?"

"You heard me."

"Who have you been talking to?"

"We've been talking to each other," Sam said. She was about as tall as Kirsty. On balance, Kirsty looked a bit meaner. Although come to think of it, it was a pretty close run thing.

"Keith, why did you invite both of us down here?"

"Well ..."

"Who are you supposed to be going out with?"

"You don't know, do you?"

"Don't care more like."

At least Keith's ankle seemed to have got much better. By now he was back on his feet and trying to engage reverse gear. The two women began advancing on him slowly in a pincer movement.

"It's time we had a chat."

"How about I call you tomorrow?"

With that they were off, all three of them heading towards the car park at a brisk pace. Fighting a rearguard action, Keith managed to talk his way off the pitch without any major incidents. By the time he reached the road we'd all started heading back to the changing rooms. Keith had wanted some support and we'd got it. The thing is, you just never know how these things are going to turn out.

"Well that's that for another week," Jerome is saying as we skirt around the rope fence protecting the cricket pitch. It's not so cold now. The sun has broken through the haze and the frost has nearly disappeared completely. When we get back to the showers the game itself has already started to recede into just another Sunday morning defeat. And by the time we've got changed it's lunchtime and there's still half a day, a quarter of a weekend, there for the taking.

A naked Nev wobbles past. Hunkered in the corner of the room, he starts to work his way through a selection of colognes and deodorants.

"Well we really should all do this again some time," he mutters. There's a bit of scattered laughter, or something close to it.

"I've heard some stupid ideas before. Today was the worst."

"Keith should be in Brighton by now."

"Promise me one thing," Dan says. "Nobody ever suggest inviting anyone down here again."

Some things really are best kept apart. Sometimes it's just not worth it. Next week we've got the Prince of Wales away in Clapham. It's still only February. It's only just starting to get cold out there. We've still got plenty of time left to save ourselves, without taking desperate measures just yet.

Personally, I'm willing to try anything. I'll do whatever it takes. Just don't ask me to share these Sunday mornings with my girlfriend, my mum or anyone else who might start wondering what we're actually doing out there. Sunday football is not a spectator sport. And much worse than the shame of losing and running around in the mud in a small pair of shorts, you might find – outside of the weekly struggle with your own limitations and our brand of broken teamwork – that there's just not that much to see.

12
Away

"What is a karma chameleon anyway?" Dan says.

"I don't know. Some kind of yoga move."

"What's a Culture Club?"

"I think it's a disco blokes with handlebar moustaches go to."

"What's anything? What's a Spandau Ballet? What's a Eurythmic?"

"A Eurythmic is definitely something. I can't remember what."

"What's a Wham?"

"Wham is a kind of sweet. Those pink chewy bars with sherbet."

There is a style of music that only exists on pub jukeboxes. A good pub jukebox will contain songs that you'd never listen to in any other situation. Frank Sinatra singing 'My Way' followed by ten minutes of Slade is not a recipe for a good night in. But add beer mats, crisps and premium lager and suddenly it starts to make a bit more sense.

"Whose round is it?"

"Michael's," Dan nods.

"Michael's broke. I'll get it."

"You're the perfect host."

"He's a perfect mug. Get more peanuts. Dry roasted."

Michael is staying with me at the moment. I've known him for nearly ten years now. He shows up with a rucksack every year or so, on his way back from America or stopping off while he waits for his visa for Thailand to come through.

"Danny boy, where are we going tonight?"

"I'm not going anywhere. It's a school night."

"Don't be like that. We're going out to meet girls."

"I can show you where the bus stop is."

Michael is Danish, although he doesn't seem to be ever in Denmark very much. As far as I can tell he's spent more time sleeping on my sofa in various flats across London over the last ten years than at home in Copenhagen. My phone rings while I'm at the bar.

"Laura."

"Where are you?"

"I'm over in the Shakespeare."

"Just as long as you're enjoying yourself, honey."

"With Michael. I thought you wanted him out of the house tonight."

"I meant with you still in it."

"Yeah. Sorry. It's just Michael wanted …"

"To go out and get pissed again. By the way, does Michael ever want to pick up his socks? Or empty his ashtrays? Just a thought."

"You know what? I'll ask him."

Michael isn't really the ideal guest. The problem is, everyone else might have moved on a bit, but he's exactly the same now as he was when we first met. He works for a few months at home every year and spends the rest of the time travelling. He smokes roll-ups and eats when he can. His hair looks like it hasn't been washed, let alone cut, since I first met him. And those manky old sun-bleached desert boots he's wearing. Could they still be the same pair?

"Cheers."

"I'm telling you, the burning man festival. It's absolutely wild. You guys will love it. It's crazy mad cool shit."

Michael learned his English mainly from American TV shows. It can be catching if you spend too much time with him.

"Everybody camps out in the desert. There's this big burning man and fireworks and everyone so wasted you wouldn't believe. It's next month. You guys have got to come."

"Yeah right."

"Unfortunately I've got a job."

"Take a holiday."

"I can't. It's all used up. I've got plans."

"What plans?"

"For the summer."

"The summer? It's March already. Get the fuck out of here."

"We're not all hippy spongers like you. I don't know enough people with free sofas."

Along with dirty jeans and the ability, still, to go without a proper shower for a few days and not really mind, Michael has something else; that willingness to put up with anything as long as at the end of it all there's a beer, a girl perhaps, and something new to look at.

Everyone has it for a while. Usually when you're about seventeen. It disappears at different times for different people. Some people can't wait to be grown up. You can see them pining for it in their early twenties, like swimmers at the end of a race reaching out for the edge of the pool. I suppose I'm in a transitional phase. But there's definitely a part of me that still wants a bit of Michael around.

"I'll put my bag down here. This is nice, much nicer than the old place with Danny boy, you've done well here, my friend, only joking, I might need to phone if that's all right, about the visa, they said to ring their office, I've tried but it takes about an hour, no good when you're in a phone box, can I use that as an ashtray, so where are we going tonight? I feel like a drink after all this work."

Laura stuck her head around the door. "Can we have a word?"

"Sure."

"In there."

Michael's visit wasn't very well timed. In fact he just sort of turned up. That's what he does.

"How long?" Laura asked.

"He said a couple of days. I can't turn him away."

"Why not?"

"He's waiting for his money to come through. He won't be any trouble."

"As I recall, he's always trouble."

"A couple of days, I promise. It's just Michael."

"Just Michael is thirty-five years old and still invading people's sofas."

"It's not an invasion."

"At least show him where the shower is."

"Yeah. I must have a word about that."

It's not just that I've known Michael for a long time, which I have. It's the way we met each other. After my A levels I left school and got a job ushering in a cinema. I'd applied to university the year before, but I didn't get in anywhere I fancied going so I let things slide. The job involved watching films all day and eating popcorn out of a plastic cup. There seemed to be a lot of time to fill and this was a good way of filling it. Dan had gone to university straight away. Nearly all of my friends had gone somewhere or other. By the end of the summer it was only really me left.

I'd heard that you could go to something called a kibbutz. My brother told me about it. He described a kibbutz as "a commune". If I'd listened more closely he might have gone on to talk about the founding ideals of shared profit and agricultural labour. Unfortunately I stopped listening at "commune", a word that made me think of people sitting around in hammocks, smoking herbal cigarettes and occasionally sleeping with each other. I booked myself a seat on a flight to Tel Aviv the following month.

Three weeks later I stepped off a bus and through the gates of a large agricultural farm in a mud-bound valley in northern Israel. It was pouring. Bent double under my rucksack, I was led to a small prefab hut with two beds. In one of them a Danish dairy farmer was asleep face down in his clothes.

My guide told me to report to the laundry at seven o'clock

the next morning and then disappeared back out into the gloom. As I stood there staring at the long brown lizard at the end of my bed, I wondered what had happened to the beautiful girls strumming guitars under the fruit trees. Where was my hammock? Clearly there had been some kind of mix-up.

For the next few weeks it rained every day. The smell of damp clothes and mouldering Portakabin attached itself to everything. Along with the other volunteers I lived in a dog-leg of paper-thin prefab huts next to a concrete bomb shelter. The huts were breezy and cool in summer. In the middle of winter they were freezing. The bathrooms were basically outdoor. It's still the only time I've ever been snowed on while taking a hot shower.

Most of the other volunteers were stopping off for a month or two as part of a trip around the world. We lived on vodka with orange squash and toast made on the two-bar fire. I had no winter clothes, but I managed to scrounge an army parka, which I wore constantly when I wasn't sleeping, or reading in bed while my Danish dairy farmer roommate slept face down in his clothes.

The days passed slowly in the laundry. I fell asleep a few times, which eventually earned me a transfer to the kitchen. Here the day started even earlier, but we finished after lunch and came slopping back in our rubber boots and overalls just as the others were going back out to the fields. The dining hall held over a thousand people and in the kitchen everything was oversized. There was a wooden spoon the size of a tennis racket, saucepans you could sit in and a silver colander like a small UFO.

This was all fine. You can get used to most things. But after a while it just wasn't enough. I needed something more. The man in the next hut down was another Dane called Michael. I'd spoken to him a couple of times, but only late at night, when his eyes had widened into two slightly mad holes framed by long blond hair on either side.

He may have been older than me, and he may have known pretty much everyone, but he also had something I wanted. Now and then I'd seen him coming back in the afternoon wearing shorts and, once, carrying a football. I caught up with him as he headed down to the laundry.

"English guy from London. Good morning."

"You're Michael. I live next door. I'm Barney."

"I know. Congratulations."

"I was wondering. Is there any football going on around here? I've seen you with your stuff."

He looked at me. "Come. Let's go. Don't worry about that. Do it later."

We wound our way through a patchwork of huts and down the side of a small orange grove to an overgrown corner where some of the longer-serving volunteers lived.

"In here."

"Michael. Where have you been?"

"With my English friend."

"Ah. God save the Queen."

A circle of long-haired Scandinavians were sat around a small table. Beer cans, a couple of vodka bottles and some bread and cheese were scattered in among the remains of a card game.

"Sit down. Have a drink. Please."

We didn't talk about anything much for the rest of the afternoon, but the next day Michael knocked on my door just as I was settling down for a siesta after work.

"Let's go."

"Where?"

"To football. Come on. Get your stuff. Before they start."

There were regular games at the far end of the kibbutz on the banks of the river. The pitch was an asphalt strip inside a metal cage, a bit like the one we used to have at primary school. The Danes had been there longest and they were in charge. On the pitch they played like the kind of pale, blond Scandinavians I'd seen on TV. Michael was bandy-legged and surprisingly quick. Together they made precise little triangles among themselves and scored neat goals. There were Swedes as well, and Germans, Israelis, a Peruvian and a couple of Japanese.

It turned out that all the footballing clichés were true. The South Americans were skilful on the ball and bad-tempered off it. The Japanese had a demented enthusiasm but were too small. Our blond German, Rolf, was commanding and technically skilled. As the sole Englishman I played my part by wellying the ball upfield as far as I could and leaping manfully for headers.

This does happen. I once played with a group of Italians in Rome. It was an evening game and at the end I started getting dressed, thinking about where to hurry off to for a drink. All around me my team-mates were heading for the showers in dressing gowns and slippers, each with his own stash of gels, soaps and moisturisers. A couple of them had hairdryers.

It was in these loose, rambling games on the asphalt pitch that my time at the kibbutz stopped feeling like a strange dream of work and broken sleep. By the time summer came around I'd made other friends too, people who didn't just drink and play football. I'd travelled around the country. I'd been to Egypt and seen the pyramids (not as big as you'd think) and I'd sat in the Pizza Hut next to the pyramids (not bad actually) with a group of girls from Leighton Buzzard.

"Hello dear, you must be hungry," my mum had said as I walked in through the front door carrying my canvas bag, straight from the airport and still smelling of mouldy showers and desert dust. It's strange how quickly you can get used to being at home again. My room at home was pretty much the same as it always had been. The house was the same. Even Lewisham looked the same. In fact, it was as though nothing had changed at all.

"You look like a dirty crusty," Dan told me the same day. I was still wearing the khaki trousers and army shoes that had seemed such a good idea halfway around the world. Dan was home from university. He had changed while I'd been away. Something about him was different. Maybe it was his new clothes or the way he kept using certain words in every sentence, like "monged" and "awesome" and "totally". Suddenly everything was totally.

"You've turned into a sad student," I told him as we waited for the night bus to New Cross.

"I live on a staircase with six girls, all with their own rooms. I know what I'm doing."

"Two to New Cross. Thanks. I can't believe I'm doing this. I've only been back a day."

"You love it."

Two stops down on the bus towards New Cross was Zeus, south-east London's largest, dirtiest night club. Everybody went to Zeus. From Thursday to Sunday it had a long and drunken queue outside it every weekend. Zeus may have been deeply uncool. It may have been a weekly mix of suburban goths and secretaries dancing to the YMCA. But it was still the only place within a ten-mile radius that was actually open after eleven o'clock at night. The important thing was never to admit that you went there, even when you were standing in the middle of the dance floor with a bottle of Hooch in each hand.

"Actually I never really come here," Dan is saying now, beneath a huge lighted sign that says, simply, ZEUS, as he pretends to dance with a very tall blonde girl wearing thigh-high boots.

"Years ago but not any more," I'm telling her friend automatically, as behind her I can see Michael trying to drag a couple of girls who could be sisters up on to the little stage at the front of the dance floor. Dan and I may be nearly thirty, but Zeus has hardly aged at all. It's still huge, crowded and very dark.

"Thank you, sir. Please stay off the stage," the muffled voice of the DJ booms through a ten-foot speaker above our heads, as Michael trips and falls backwards on to the floor.

"I thought you said this was a school night."

"Yeah, I thought so too. Anyway you've got a wife at home. What are you doing here?"

"I'm not married. I don't know what I'm doing here."

There didn't seem much point in going home early. Laura had already lost patience with me. It was probably when she rang to say goodnight and I told her to wait a second, we were nearly up to five pounds on the quiz machine. Michael appears out of the crowd with a triangle of pint glasses clamped between his palms.

"This club is wild. How come you never mentioned it before?"

"It's Dan's place really. Look, Michael, I'd better go. You can find your own way back."

"No, stay. Don't go home."

"Why not?"

"Because when are you going to see me again?"

"Six months from now probably."

"Hold my beer. Watch this."

Michael wanders into a small space that has appeared on the dance floor. After a while he starts turning in small circles, gathering his strength.

"He's going to do it."

"What?"

"The backspin."

Dropping on to one knee, he launches himself into a sudden breakdance pirouette, drawing his legs up to his chest and spinning around on his back in a tight bundle on the beaten wood floor. People turn to look. Someone points and laughs. As he starts to slow Michael lifts a leg to balance himself and hoofs a heavy pint glass off a table. It shatters and the pieces are sent spinning away across the dance floor. Just as quickly he's up on his feet. There's a black smudge on the back of his white T-shirt as he starts apologising.

"What a muppet."

"He's going to get his head kicked in."

"Oh shit."

But instead of fists and raised voices something else is happening. Michael has got his arm around a small dark girl. She laughs as he gives her his drink, which he's grabbed back from Dan.

"Oh my God."

"He's pulled with a backspin."

"I've never seen that before."

"Maybe we can go home now."

Strange things do happen when Michael's around. He's just one of those people, I suppose. On the kibbutz we used to play football every day. The games tended to blur into one after a while. Despite this there is one particular afternoon that's always stuck with me.

We started at about four o'clock, an eleven-a-side of North vs. South, shirts vs. skins. This basically meant Scandinavia, Germany and England (me) against the rest. The pitch was large and crumbling and tucked away from everything else by the river. It seemed to get bigger the longer you were out there. There weren't any tall buildings around or even any trees nearby, so most of the time when you looked up all you saw above the high wire fence was the sky. After fifteen minutes it was so hot we were down to skins on both sides.

The game started quickly. We didn't take any breaks. After an hour the score was 17–15. Rolf rounded the keeper to make it 18–15. A few minutes later Jose, a Costa Rican, pulled one back for the South and went off to collapse on the touchline.

"Off and on when you want. Keep it moving," someone called out as one of the local kids who had been watching ran on to take his place. With the score 28–26 to the North, the sun had already started to sink down below the mountains. After ten minutes of stalemate our Italian Paulo scored with a shot that pinged in off a post – 29–26 – and I noticed a crowd had gathered to watch on the sidelines. Despite the gloom nobody was showing any signs of slowing down just yet. Already there was an understanding between us. This was a long way from being over.

Still the speed of the game refused to slow. At 35–37, with the sun just a pink tinge above the hills and the sky turning a deep blue, Michael came running back on with his knee freshly bandaged and I realised my whole team had been replaced, one by one, from its original line-up. My legs felt weirdly light and heavy at the same time. The air was cold around us and it freshened you up just moving through it.

Whenever our momentum started to slow something would always happen to pick it up again. For a while a group of Mexicans almost took over the game, tilting it right back towards the South. The Mexicans were small and skilful. They didn't run much, but they kept the ball away from the rest of us. In twenty minutes they scored four or five times without reply, but they lost momentum after one of them went off the pitch with a bruised ankle.

I spent half an hour in attack, swapping with Michael, then half an hour in defence, and twenty minutes in goal. By now, with the sky almost black and the only light an orange glow from the farm buildings nearby, we'd all gradually changed into shirts and jumpers. A couple of South players had head-scarves on. Didier, a Frenchman, was wearing gloves. There still didn't seem to be any reason to stop.

"No free kicks any more. Keep it going," a voice called out as we moved cautiously forward. Underneath the tiredness, the goal-hanging and missed kicks, a new code of conduct had begun to emerge. You could shout for a foul if you wanted (no one bothered) and whoever was nearest could go in goal (known as monkey rush at home; don't ask me why). There were factions emerging, mini-games within the game, one-on-one duels. At one point I joined a small crowd watching as Michael and Henrik, both Danes, wrestled in the folds of the fence. As they were separating I spotted the ball being ferried around over on the far side of the pitch.

The game finally came to an end close to midnight. For a while things had been in slow decline. Players had begun to sit down when the ball was at the other end. Some of us were wearing coats. There was a semi-serious scuffle between Kaszuo, our Japanese, and an Australian called Shane.

"Last goal wins it," someone shouted and, despite the tiredness, for the next ten minutes we went at it with fresh legs. The South almost scored twice, our keeper André pulling off a save at point-blank range with players around me already cele-brating. The North hit a post. Eventually we settled into ten minutes of cagey cat-and-mouse before, finally, with the cold starting to bite, Michael appeared in the orange light around the South goal to slide the ball past a diving keeper. He almost lapped the pitch in celebration, half the team following him and half just sitting down where they were on the concrete.

My first reaction was huge relief at winning the game, a feeling I'd never have thought possible in a kickabout on a gravelly pitch, close to midnight, against a group of blokes wearing gloves and hats. My second and third thoughts were, what the hell am I doing out here at this time in the freezing cold, totally knackered, with two grazed knees and blood dripping from my left elbow? And, come to think of it, isn't it two-for-one vodka night in the disco at the chicken coop near the bomb shelter? Despite this, one thing was clear. That this was a proper game of football. It was also the kind of thing that happens, not always, but now and then, if you hang around for long enough with someone like Michael.

"What's happened to him?" I say, peering towards the dark corners of the Zeus dance floor.

"He was upstairs the last time I saw him," Dan shrugs. "He must have gone back somewhere."

"Oh well. It might do me a favour not having anyone on the sofa tonight."

Dan and I decide to share a taxi home, north to his flat and then west out to Shepherd's Bush. I have to admit, I didn't spend too long looking for Michael. I was ready to go home hours ago. I really can't be hanging around places like Zeus. I'm not single. I'm not going through a period of experimentation with my body's alcohol capacity. There is, literally, no point.

"Zeus really is shit."

"Yeah," Dan agrees. "Although to be honest I never went there much."

"I'm not going back. This is it for me. It's the straight and narrow from now on."

At home the lights are turned off and the house is dark. This is a good sign. The living room is empty, with Michael's things neatly folded on the sofa. I get into bed straight away, seeking out the warmth under the duvet after the chill of catching a cab in freezing New Cross, and lie there for a moment or two enjoying the feeling of being home.

"You smell of cigarettes," Laura says in a muffled voice, moving closer.

"Sorry. Sorry about earlier."

"It's okay. It was just a surprise."

There's the faintest rumble of a car from the main road and maybe the start of rain flickering against the bedroom window as we both drift off to sleep. The night is still a difficult one, though. Maybe I drank too much. I suppose I didn't really eat anything either. Whatever the reason, sleep is broken and fitful. It's as though some echo of the club is still beating somewhere inside my head. Morning arrives just in time.

I wander through to the kitchen. Maybe I'll take Laura some tea in bed. I probably should after last night. There's still a faint smell of smoke. It must be something left on my clothes, although that seems a bit unlikely, and there's a creaking sound from somewhere and I'm thinking, okay, Michael must have made it back after all, as I open the door to the living room and realise, oh yes, he made it back all right. Hearing Laura's familiar step I close the door quickly behind me.

"Don't come in here."

"What?"

"Just wait a second."

Michael is no longer on the sofa. He's sprawled across the floor in the middle of a haystack of blankets and pillows. There's music playing and glasses and bottles are scattered across every surface. He's not alone. Not one but two extra sets of limbs are visible under his blanket. He raises his head and smiles.

"Hey. What happened to you guys last might?"

"What the fuck is this?"

"This is Charlene and Jade."

A face appears from under the duvet. "Hi."

"Hello. Michael, there's crap everywhere. And red wine all over the sofa. And fucking fag butts."

"What's going on?" The door handle turns behind me and I tighten my grip on it.

"You wanker," I hiss. "I'm already in trouble and then you go and do this."

"We'll clear up. Hey, come on."

The other bodies in the bed stir reluctantly. There's a click of something being replaced that sounds like a receiver.

"Have you been on the phone?"

"Oh right, that was me? Michael said it would be okay?" Charlene says in an Australian accent.

"Who's in the bathroom?" Laura says from outside.

"Who's in the fucking bathroom?"

"Nadia."

"Who the fuck is Nadia?"

"Nice girl. From Zeus."

The door opens finally and Laura stands there in her dressing gown taking a long look around. She almost laughs.

"Hello, Michael. Nice to see you're feeling at home."

"Hey, I'm sorry," he calls out.

"I'm going into the bathroom and then I'm going to work," she says quietly. "When I come home I want this place back to normal. And you'd better be out of here."

She heads down the corridor and into the bathroom as somebody wearing just a towel, presumably Nadia, pads past.

"Listen, buddy, I think you better make it up to her. She's pretty mad," Michael says, rolling out of bed in his tie-dye shorts and starting to make an effort at straightening things up. I sit down in an armchair and knock over a pile of CDs with my foot.

"You might be right. For once I think you actually might be right."

13
The worst game of football
I've ever played in my life

Sunday March 8th 2005
Mail Coach Inn vs. Bolingbroke Athletic

The light through the living-room window wakes me up. The first thing I see is a full ashtray six inches from my nose. The second thing is a jar of Marmite with a knife sticking out of the top. In the kitchen there's no proper food in the fridge, just Diet Coke, cheese and lots of dark chocolate. After three months away it's good to be back. I'm drinking coffee and reading an American magazine about wrestling when Dan finally emerges in his dressing gown.

"I got that on the plane back from Chicago. Wrestling. It's not what it used to be."

"It's definitely more suntanned. You don't see any hairy blokes in leotards."

"It's like porn. They've gone the same way. It used to be home-made and out of shape. Now it's all airbrushed and American."

"They do a lot more shouting these days."

"I never really listen to what they're saying."

"I mean in the wrestling. What time is it?"

"Nine. We'd better get going soon."

He stares at the wall. His eyes mist over. He seems to be doing some kind of calculation.

"Oh shit. Spring forward, fall back. The clocks changed last night. It's ten."

"Of course it is. Fuck. Why don't I ever remember that?"

"They always have it on a Sunday. Who does anything important on a Sunday morning?"

"Only idiots."

"And people who go to church."

We're out of the door in five minutes. Dan is still in his pyjamas. He's carrying a bag of boots and socks, a slab of Cheddar and a cigarette.

"Keith's going to kill us."

"We've got twenty minutes. We'll make it."

"Remind me. Why do we do this again?"

It's March now and we haven't won a game since September. Not that this, in itself, is a problem. Most of the time it's enough just to get eleven players out on the field and stage something that at least looks a bit like a football match. There's been no shortage of effort. But there's realism too; not to mention a losing streak that stretches back to when the days were still getting colder and shorter rather than lighter and warmer. Even at times like these, games will appear that you feel you can win. There are always days when hope starts to flutter. These are the dangerous games.

Our opponents, the Mail Coach Inn, are bottom of the league. Which is another way of saying they're below us. The game should be closely fought. There's nothing to fear in the opposition, no skill shortfall or individual battle we can't hope to win. We're three-quarters of the way through the season. I've got a cricked knee, a twanged hamstring and a sore neck. Despite all of this, there's still a sense that the season might turn around for us. Hope, unfortunately, springs eternal.

I've been at Dan's for a couple of days. Ever since the Michael incident, in fact. It almost feels like going home, despite the fact that what was once my room is now being used for storage by one of Dan's workmates who's been transferred to Eindhoven for six months. Almost like home, but not quite.

Last night we went out drinking. This was Dan's way of making me feel better. He took me to drown my sorrows in some bars that just happened to be full of apparently un-attached young women. Back at the flat I made up a spare bed on the fat leather sofa.

"That was fun," Dan said, yawning.

"I suppose so."

"You know, if I was you I wouldn't be here. I'd be with Laura begging her to forgive me."

"It wasn't me in bed with three girls from Zeus."

"Yeah, but it was your mate. And all the other crap might have had a little bit to do with it."

"I said sorry."

"Well say it again. Tell her you're a changed man."

"Am I?"

"I don't know. Just say it."

I haven't moved out. I'm just taking a breather, letting the dust settle. How long, do you think, before it's settled? We just need some time to cool down. And some time for Laura to decide she wants to start talking to me again. I haven't really had time to think since Friday, what with work and football and more football. Sometimes it does have its uses.

At least Michael left straight away. Kicking him out turned out to be the easiest thing in the world. I think he'd been expecting it for a couple of days. He was already packed and ready to leave. The last I saw of him he was off with his backpack and his A–Z, hunting down some other long-lost mate with a vacant armchair or living-room floor.

The game is in Wimbledon, somewhere on a large, wind-blown playing field on the fringes of the motorway. We're in Dan's brother's van. He's got a furniture shop in Kennington. The van is a long Transit with an outline of a chandelier on the side, although I've never seen any chandeliers in the shop. I've got a map spread out on my knees as we crawl through the Sunday morning gridlock. It's not that London never sleeps. Sometimes it seems as though it never really wakes up.

"There might be a short cut if we can get through the next set of lights."

"Forget about it. There are no short cuts. You know that."

Dan is brushing his teeth as he drives. He rinses his mouth with a bottle of water.

"Have you ever wondered why there are so many different types of toothbrush?"

"No."

"There are, though. There are hundreds of them. All shapes and colours. You'd think someone would decide which one actually worked and leave it at that."

"Maybe they all do."

"They can't all work. They're completely different. Do you get an angled head? A round head? Firm, medium or soft?"

"I always get firm. Firm lasts longer."

"Of course. What kind of person buys medium?"

Heavy raindrops spatter the windscreen as we lurch through an orange light and join the queue for the motorway.

"Shouldn't we get some petrol?" I say, noticing the needle on red. "There's a garage coming up."

"We've started moving now."

"Yeah but it's on empty."

"This thing can go for fifty miles on red. We'll be fine."

A part of me wouldn't mind if we never made it anyway. Sometimes it's hard to remember exactly why we're so bothered about saving this football team. As we join the stream of traffic going south the buildings melt away and a hedgerow opens out into a field, a reservoir and a distant line of trees. Dirty black clouds scud across the horizon and there's a shaft of cold sunlight through a patch of pale blue.

"You know how, generally, things are supposed to get better?"

"Yeah. If you say so," Dan murmurs, changing lanes.

"Well, you just assume they will."

"Perhaps."

"Maybe they need to get really bad first."

"What are you talking about?"

"I've just got a feeling about today."

"What did that sign say? Fuck. I think it said left."

Jittery now, we make our way along the dual carriageway, scanning the side of the road for some indication that we might be heading the right way. Fifteen minutes later we're careering into the car park at Wimbledon after almost losing ourselves for ever in an out-of-town Asda. Fighting the dry, throbbing sensation behind my eyes, I jog across the gravel towards the edge of a brick pavilion that appears through a gap in the poplar trees.

The sounds of the road disappear behind us and suddenly it's like a different world. A huge expanse of green reaches away to a hilly horizon. Goalposts fleck the horizon where tiny figures walk in twos and threes towards the distant corners. By the club-house kits of all colours, sizes and eras mingle. As we scan the shirts for a familiar white and blue, Keith appears in front of us.

"Five minutes," he says. "Take the key and lock up. You'd better get out there quick."

"Where are we?"

"Pitch two. Fuck knows where that is. Just look for the yellows and whites."

"Should be a close one today."

"It could have been. We've only got nine."

"Nine?"

"Something about the clocks. And Dave's in France."

"France?"

"Something about half-term."

"Half-term?"

"Something about the kids."

"Kids?"

"Just get in there and get changed."

Pitch two is in the far corner. We jog past an endlessly repli-
cating stream of Sunday footballers: a clutch of goalkeepers
sitting on a bench, a pair of referees standing by a noticeboard.
Above us bruised clouds ferry rain across the sky. Lars is
stringing up the nets. Simon and Nev are kicking a ball around
in the centre circle. We look even less than nine out here in the
open. Behind the far goal front gardens peek through the gaps
in the fence. A row of brittle winter trees lines the far side.
Keith is standing with the Hawk, watching the yellow shirts
warm up in the far goal.

"You know what? We really should be beating this lot."

Keith's eyes are glazed this morning and he looks like he
hasn't shaved for a few days. Nev is sitting down cross-legged
on the touchline. Next to him Jerome is still wearing his coat
and his scarf.

"Big effort today. This could be it for us. If we can get our
act together," Keith says.

"Why don't you have a word? Everyone listens to you,"
Dan tells him.

"You think so?"

"Yeah. You've got a really loud grating voice."

As we gather around the halfway line. I notice Charlie is
wearing a blue and white tracksuit top and a blue and white
bobble hat.

"Is that Bolingbroke colours?"

"You can get them in Larkhall Sports."

"Nice."

"Did you go down with your mum?" Jerome asks.

"No," he says, in a way that suggests it might have been a near thing.

"All right, lads," Keith says, clapping his hands. "We've got nine fit men so let's give it everything. We can beat this lot. This could be the season for us."

He looks around eagerly. There's an awkward silence.

"All right, Keith, but let's not get too hung up on it. It's only a game."

"Meaning what?"

"Meaning we're meant to be enjoying this."

"Like I say, if we can give it a big first fifteen ..."

"That's just it though, isn't it?" Charlie interrupts suddenly. "Some of us don't really want to win. Some of us wouldn't be too upset if we didn't carry on next year."

"We're here, aren't we? Of course we want to carry on," Lucien says.

"So how did we get in this position in the first place?"

"By being shit."

"Lads, lads, lads," Keith says, holding his hands up. "As I was saying, we've got nine of us. So we're playing one up front, four across the middle. Midfield, get up to support Bob when we can, keep those two banks of four ..."

"Banks of four. It's always the same bollocks," Simon mutters.

"It's not bollocks. It's tactics."

"Keith, you don't know anything about tactics. That's why we keep losing."

"Listen, Goth boy ..."

"I'm not a Goth," Lucien says.

"Of course you are."

"No, I'm not."

"What's all the black for then?"

"What black?"

"Your clothes. Your hair."

"If you must know, my hair is aubergine."

"Er, lads. When you're ready."

The referee is short and dapper. His outfit matches his salt-and-pepper hair and moustache. Behind him the opposition are already standing lined up in formation ready to kick off.

"Sorry, ref."

"Come on then, lads."

"Big first ten, whites."

The pitch looks lopsided. It slips away gently down towards the rows of goals that unravel away to our left. A raw wind gusts across, threatening to blow us overboard and all the way down to the tiny trees and fences at the far end. Today I'm playing next to Simon in midfield. He stands ignoring me with his cuffs over his wrists as a squall of freezing rain spatters the mud at our feet.

"You all right?" I ask him.

"Yeah, why?"

"You sounded a bit pissed off."

"Why don't you ask Dan?"

"What?"

"I said ask Dan."

The game starts slowly. The ball seems to want to leave the

field as much as possible, propelled into the distance by the wind and some booming clearances from both defences. For a few minutes we look like what we are, two losing teams cowed by the prospect of a season-saving victory.

I know why we don't win many games. The reason is: we aren't very good. The most obvious excuse is lack of practice. There's also our lack of fitness, too many of us discovering that things only get harder as you get near your thirties. And recently there's been a feeling that we're pulling against each other, making ourselves less than the sum of our parts. Today our losing streak has taken on a distinctive character. You can almost see it, following us like a black cloud.

The green and yellow shirts look different. They've got more spiky haircuts and blond highlights than I've seen all season. They're younger than us and there's an absence of settled gut and brawny neck. They don't talk to each other in the same way either. There's less shouting and definitely less swearing. On the plus side, I can see them being left twitching in the mud by any self-respecting bunch of Daves with number two crops and a convoy of white vans in the car park.

A lofted clearance by Keith sails over the touchline, pogo-ing away on the wind and clearing the game on the next pitch until the ball is just a white speck in the distance.

"What's wrong with Simon?" I say to Dan.

"I don't know what's wrong with him."

"He said to ask you."

"I don't know. Ask Sally."

Sally is Simon's sister. She was at Halfmarshes last week. Something clicks.

"Oh no, you didn't. Tell me you didn't."

"I didn't do much, that's for sure. What does he care anyway?"

"I can think of a few reasons. You for a start. And your long-term girlfriend."

"Bollocks."

"TURN AND FACE, BOLINGBROKE."

"Take a man. TAKE A FUCKING MAN."

There's a frazzled edge to the shouts as we defend a meandering attack. Nev attempts a hacked clearance near the corner flag. The ball ricochets to Keith, who blasts it against Nev and out of play.

"Give me a name."

"Runners! Watch the runners!"

The ball bobbles free in midfield and there's a volley of shouting, familiar voices stretched by a note of hysteria. We fall back to defend a free kick on the left touchline and I find myself being yelled at from both sides.

"Number seven's free!"

"Stay on your man!"

Charlie glares at me, a look of total outrage on his face as he stomps one of his short legs into the turf and jabs a finger in my direction.

"DON'T WALK AWAY! GET BACK IN THERE!" he screams. The sky has darkened, the clouds turning a deeper shade of grey, and the wind seems to be coming from every direction at once. We're all on edge today. There are no final straws. Today every straw is the final straw.

As half-time looms, after forty-five minutes played out to a shapeless timpani of orders and threats, something finally happens. Finding space on the far side, a yellow-shirted delegation launches a raid on the edge of our penalty area. The ball finally bobbles through to Lars who takes a huge slow motion swing at it and scuffs his clearance to a yellow shirt ten yards out. A tall number eleven is left with the simple task of smashing it gleefully into an empty net.

"Heads up, boys," Keith says as we trudge back for the restart, but there's no time. The half-time whistle comes suddenly. As the rain starts to fall again we form a drooping huddle on the touchline.

There's a pattern to most things. Playing football should be exciting. If Sunday football was a film it ought to be *Gladiator*, or at the very least *Zulu*. Of course, most of the time it's nothing like that. Usually by half-time it feels like *Reservoir Dogs*, a bunch of losers holed up in a warehouse with the sirens closing in. Today we've lost even the camaraderie of the bungled bank robbery. We've taken a step even further down the scale. Today we're a plunging jet plane, a burning building, a sinking ship with a cast of has-beens fighting it out over the lifeboats. Nev lies down with his head on his soaking bag and shuts his eyes. Charlie stands stiffly off to one side.

"Lads, we're still in this …"

"Oh bollocks."

"Keith, the only thing we're still in is the fucking rain."

"Lads, listen …"

"Why won't you listen? Why don't you care? You're all bastards. All of you."

Charlie is standing apart from us. He takes a step back, clenching his fists.

"Charlie, take it easy."

"No, I won't take it easy. Why does everyone want to take it easy?"

"He's fucking lost it."

"Charlie, mate, sort it out. It's only football," Dan says, smiling.

"Oh yeah. People are funny, aren't they?" Simon mutters.

"What's that supposed to mean?"

"It's easy when you're just having a laugh."

Pointedly, Dan walks away. Behind him Keith has got his arm around Charlie's shoulders. They're both talking at the same time. Bob is standing off to one side looking very cold. Lucien and Lars are arguing about whose fault the goal was. Jerome is sitting on his own with his coat around his shoulders. I sit down next to him in the mud.

"What do you reckon?"

"Not a lot."

"I notice you managed to stay out of all that."

"I've got nothing to say, that's why."

"Why not?"

"Because it's bollocks. You all act like the team is such a big deal but you don't even enjoy it. You're too slow and too unfit to do anything anyway. Whatever you're doing here it's not about making it work. So what's the point of arguing?"

I take a drink from his bottle of water.

"Yeah. That sounds about right."

Brian Clough said it only takes a second to put the ball in the onion bag. That can't be right. A shot from the edge of the box would reach the net in just under a second. Before then it has to be set up. Add more time for celebrations, defensive inquests and being booked for waving your shirt around your head. And in reality it probably takes about two minutes to put the ball in the onion bag. This season it took us much longer than that: three whole games to score our first goal. Now we need two more, just to turn around a game we should, finally, be winning.

I spend the first five minutes of the second half chasing the ball down. Dragged by the slope and the wind the game settles in my corner of the pitch. As I run back to help Dan by the corner flag, taking small steps on the rutted surface, I feel something snap at the top of my leg. Suddenly I can't run. My left side has seized up completely, leaving me hopping on one leg.

I felt a tightness there earlier. I'd been too jittery to stretch properly, hoping it would just ping itself loose in the way muscles sometimes do. Juddering to a halt I wave my arms and cry out as the ball is ferried past. Nobody notices. I manage to stumble over the touchline, pain gripping my left side.

"I've done my leg. Give me a few minutes," I shout at Keith. There's some Deep Heat in one of the bags so I rub it into the tendon. The rain makes it drip and run. I watch for a few minutes, feeling a crazy kind of guilt as the pain gives way to a gentle throb. I can feel the pull of the game again, a part of me remembering our hopeful talk. *We've got to be beating this lot.* Not with eight men, we won't. Fuck it. I throw my jacket down and run back on.

"I can't run. I'll do what I can."

Keith doesn't seem to hear. But still better to be in the thick of it than on the sidelines, the scapegoat we all seem to have been looking for. For me the next thirty minutes are pure purgatory. Reduced to a jangling, hunchbacked gallop, I hop around the centre circle, pathetically exposed, bypassed, snubbed. After a scuffle near the corner flag we win a throw-in. Simon wanders across to take it. Nobody moves as he waves the ball around behind his head, skinny wrists clenched.

"Come on, then."

Eventually Dan runs towards him. Coiling himself backwards, Simon flexes his knees and hurls it straight into Dan's face. The ball catches the side of his head as he ducks.

"What the fuck was that?"

"A throw-in."

"You did that on purpose."

As Simon jogs back into position Dan kicks a clump of mud at him off the bottom of his boot, just like we used to do at school. It makes a slapping sound as it hits his thigh. He reaches out a hand and pushes Dan hard in the chest.

"What the fuck are you doing?"

"Oi. You two. Cut it out."

But it's too late. Dan and Simon are squaring up. Fighting might be a bit of an exaggeration. Tall and spidery, Simon tries to connect with a series of haymakers. Dan is quicker but more cowardly. He manages to avoid the blows while giving an unconvincing impression of being about to wade in himself. Eventually Simon lands a weak punch to his ear.

"Shit. Sorry."

"What do you mean, sorry? You attacked me."

The Hawk has appeared by now. Expertly he grabs Simon in what looks like a judo hold.

"Easy, boys."

"Aargh. That really hurts."

"Let's all calm down now."

"Get off. Aargh."

The referee manages to squeeze himself in between them.

"Lads, I'll give you one warning," he says. "Take this back to the changing rooms or let's all get on with the game right now."

Simon looks at Dan. "Er, get on with the game?"

"I suppose so."

A few years ago I saw a huge fight on the next pitch while I was playing a game on Blackheath. It was like a brawl in a Western. After about five minutes the main free-for-all dissolved into a few wheezing one-on-ones and then finally just two blokes still trying to throttle each other. It wasn't a bad tackle that started it or an elbow. These were players on the same team, men in the same colour shirt running twenty yards to launch a sneaky punch or a flying kick while the opposition stood and watched. Fights between footballers are rare, but when they do happen they're often domestics.

As time ticks away the game has become eerily calm again. I feel like I'm leaving parts of me behind all over the pitch, tottering about in the eye of the storm. Stretched now and undermanned, our defence has started to unravel. A corner from the left is curled in towards the centre spot, where a thatch of spiky blond hair rises to head the ball firmly into the net.

The second goal kills us. Even the irritation vanishes out of our game. There's silence as the ball is rolled back towards the centre circle. A shameful sense of relief floats around the pitch as the final whistle blows. This time there's no pause for hand-shakes. We turn and walk back towards the dressing room, strung out in single file like strangers on a busy pavement. Inside I take my boots off and hobble through the throng of weary figures. The room is silent. Charlie sits in a far corner, head down. As I lower myself on to the bench, Keith claps me on the shoulder.

"Here he is. The fucking martyr."

Just for a second I love him for it. The sky has closed in by the time we pull out of the car park. Headlights wink past in the opposite direction. I'm sitting in between Dan and Simon along the front seat. Whatever happened back there, it seems to have cleared the air. These things never really last long.

"Well, that wasn't great," Dan says.

"It wasn't the best," Simon agrees. He passes me a packet of custard creams.

"These things taste like cardboard."

"You have to forget about that. Just give in to them."

We've got the heater on full blast as the traffic on the motorway concertinas out into a grudging gallop.

"I wouldn't say it wasn't the best exactly," I say, chewing a biscuit. "I'd go further than that. I'd say that was without doubt the worst game of football I've ever played in my life."

"You didn't enjoy yourself, then."

"Add in the hangover, my knackered leg and the fact that all day I just wanted to be at home persuading my girlfriend not to dump me, and it's probably right up there with the most miserable afternoons of my life."

The rain has started to drum on the metal roof again.

"Well, like you said earlier, maybe we've had the bad bit."

"Things get better now, do they?"

"Why not? They can't get any worse."

"No. I suppose not."

And come to think of it maybe Dan's right. What have we got to fear? I'll go home and talk to Laura. Football can sort itself out. We're all still friends. It's warm in the van. Even the road looks quite pretty as the traffic streams past on the other side.

"Anyway, there's always next week. Oh shit."

"What?"

"I don't know."

"Why are we stopping?"

"I don't know."

"I thought you said we could go fifty miles on empty."

"We can. It all depends where you start from."

The van splutters its final breath as we creep on to the hard shoulder. Outside the cars trundle past. Nobody moves for a while.

"The AA," Dan says at last.

"Are you a member?"

"We can join."

My leg has started hurting again. It throbs when I sit still.

Moving isn't any better. It's getting dark outside now, an eerie blue light still lingering above the trees.

"Right. The guy says wait by the side of the road so they can see us."

"How long will it be?"

"He couldn't say. An hour maybe."

Outside there's a muddy verge and a sign about caring for the countryside. We find a concrete pillar and sit down facing the motorway.

"That's not so bad, is it?" Dan says, zipping his jacket up to his chin.

"Quite nice really," Simon says from inside his hood.

Across six lanes of traffic there's a distant cluster of buildings on the other side of the road.

"That's a pub over there."

Through lighted windows I can just about make out people sitting at tables. There's an open fire further in.

"That looks warm."

"You go. I'll wait."

"No. Let's all stick together."

"We'd never get across anyway."

Next to the pub there's a café. A family walk out through the sliding doors and a warm glow spreads across the pavement outside.

"What was the problem with Laura then?" Dan says, changing the subject as a high-sided lorry rumbles past, sending up a fine spray.

"Oh nothing. Football. Me. I'll sort it out."

"It's not easy."

"No. It isn't."

It's almost dark by now. The headlights snake through the trees and over the prow of the hill, creeping towards us like a giant caterpillar. The rain has stopped and the sky is clear. A lorry pulls out of the car park across the road, catching us full in its glare.

"Beers," Dan says. "Amstel."

"Budweiser," Simon mutters.

"Carlsberg."

"Er... Draught Guinness."

"Is that a drink?"

"Of course it is. It comes in a different can."

"It's not a beer. It's a stout."

"What's the difference?"

"Lager's fizzy. Bitter's weak and flat. Ale's brown. Stout's thick."

"Animals then. Anteater."

"Bee."

"B what?"

"Just bee. Anteater's a stupid name for an animal. It's just called what it eats. Nothing else is named after its food."

"Except for woodpecker."

"Now you're back on drinks again."

By the time the truck with the orange flashing light pulls up we've already been through the alphabet three times.

14
Keeping it together

American Hot. Four Seasons. Margarita. You know where you are with pizzas. They come in familiar shapes. You can give them other names if you want to, but it all boils down to the same line-up. Experiments always seem a bit gimmicky. I once bought a frozen baked bean pizza for a laugh. I ate it, but it really wasn't very funny.

"How did people cope before they invented supermarkets?"

"They spent hours cooking," Dan says.

"Or their wives did. Imagine a world with no pasta. No fish fingers."

"Just corned beef."

There's a cutting edge to fast food in London. Things move quickly. For ages Mr Slice, the pizza delivery place near the flat, was the cheapest around. We used to feel a bit low-down ordering from him so often.

These days Mr Slice is getting respectable. It's not that he's on the up. There's just more stuff down at the bottom end. Chicken Castle and Chicken Chalet have both moved in. Worst of all, the £1.99 Diner has appeared. I walked past it earlier today. Everything costs £1.99, from hot dog, to burger, to six chicken barbecue nuggets. Up the road somebody has just opened a £2.99 Express. Presumably for those really special evenings when only the best will do.

Today we played it safe and stuck to Mr Slice. His cardboard boxes are scattered across the fat leather sofa that will become my bed again later tonight. It's been a week now of dossing at Dan's flat. Clearly, these things take time.

"Turn it over. I can't watch *EastEnders*," he says.

"What do you mean, you can't?"

"It does my head in. All these people living in the same square, going to the same pub year after year. It's like a nightmare."

"I stopped watching when they started having famous people. Even the bloke who used to be Tucker in *Grange Hill* was too much. You'd recognise him straight away. How can you believe in a place where no one has ever watched *Grange Hill*?"

"Barbara Windsor worked behind the bar."

"Exactly. No one in the square has seen the *Carry On* films? Come off it."

"Dynamo Kiev-Valencia is starting anyway."

I've got my laptop still open on my knee. This is work for me. Or it was, until I stopped doing anything constructive shortly after lunch. Dan came home at six, sat down on the sofa and still hasn't moved. All that's happened is the room has got messier around him.

"We should have had curry. I haven't eaten any vegetables all week."

"Missing home cooking?"

"That and other things."

"So what are you doing scabbing around here? No offence."

"It's not the right time to go back. Not yet."

"How do you know?"

"She told me. It's not just the thing with Michael. This has been brewing for a while. She said she wants to know where we're going."

"What is it with women? They've always got to be going somewhere. It might be worth just saying sorry."

"I have. Sort of."

"I'd start with that. A proper, no-holds-barred apology. No mucking about. Like Elton John said, sometimes sorry seems to be the hardest word."

"You're probably right."

Actually, I have always quite liked Elton John. Not so much because of his music, no offence Elton. More because of his bizarre, tantrum-filled life. And, of course, because of his football.

"I was cocaine addicted," Elton once admitted, of his years of excess. "I was an alcoholic. I had a sexual addiction. I was bulimic for six years. For breakfast I'd have a fry-up followed by twenty pots of cockles and then a tub of Häagen-Dazs vanilla ice cream."

And there we were thinking Mr Slice was a bit stodgy. But forget the cockles. The oddest thing about Elton's life was his relationship with Watford and Graham Taylor. Elton came from a football family. His cousin Roy Dwight broke his leg playing in the FA Cup Final. He became a director of Watford in 1974 and under him the club rose to an all-time high. They were good for each other. What Elton really needed back then was a steadying influence. He found one in football and in Taylor, the manager he hired.

"For a period I was his reality," Taylor said later. They made an odd couple. This was before football became a branch of the light entertainment industry. There weren't any other pop stars having heart-to-hearts in the players' lounge. It was just Elton, with his pastel-coloured safari helmet, his candy-striped walking cane and his genuine love of Watford Football Club.

Eventually, funnelled through rehab and dry-out, Elton got back on the rails. He's still with us, and looking better than ever in the right light. Football doesn't always get credit for some of the good things it does. It has a bad reputation. As does Graham Taylor.

"I was just saying to your colleague, the referee's got me the sack. Thank him ever so much for that, won't you?"

Taylor spluttered these words into the ear of a passing official on the touchline at the De Kuip stadium over ten years ago now, as Holland were beating his England team to qualify for the 1994 World Cup.

Watching at home in the living room of my small and very dirty student house, I wasn't surprised to see things go wrong. It was a bleak time. There was something wrong with the national game. Some kind of talent blockage had taken hold.

Confusion reigned at every level. One thing seemed clear. It all started with the man at the top.

During his time as England manager Taylor became a bit of a national joke. He was like an embarrassing uncle who somehow ended up with the second most important job in the country. Despite this, I always quite liked him. Managers had always been called things like Don, Johnny, Ronnie, Ron and Ray. All these Rons and Dons, unsmiling men in hats, had seemed interchangeable when I was growing up. Taylor was an outsider. As late as 1994 he still looked like a chirpy scoutmaster with a pocket full of bread for the ducks.

In the end nobody was very surprised to see him fail. To me it was a fitting accompaniment to my own lack of direction. I was twenty years old and in the middle of my second year at university.

Nobody does much while they're a student. Even people suspected of ant-like dedication to their studies are usually only guilty of putting in the odd morning in the library. In the middle of this I managed to take laziness to an extreme. That year I didn't go to a single lecture. For a whole term I failed to turn up to any of my tutorials. At one point in our house we had a sweepstake on who could avoid any kind of contact with the university for the longest period of time. I won, staying away for twenty-seven days in a row.

It was a strange year. Within a few weeks of the start of term I'd reached a point of zero momentum. I'd just run out of juice. I didn't want to be anywhere, least of all in a panelled library studying feminist historicism. I shared a house with Justin, Matt and Mike. I was doing English. They were doing things like Chemistry and Engineering, subjects that involved moping around a huge modern laboratory block on the far side of town.

We lived in a small house in a row of terraces surrounded by canals on all sides. There were four of us sharing, although at times we could have been a whole army of moonlighting dustmen. We watched Graham Taylor arguing with the Swiss linesman on the TV in our fag-brown living room, surrounded by a private landfill of rubbish that never got cleared up, a carpet of dust that never got hoovered and piles of dishes that never got done. By the end of first term we had mice, rats, cockroaches and beetles. Even the water from the taps in the bathroom looked like it could do with a good scrub.

A lot of the squalor probably had something to do with Mike. He was that kind of student. He knew people from the town, men with lank hair and unhealthy dogs on bits of string. Mike's hobby was smoking weed. Not just rolling it up. Not even simply putting it in a pipe. This wasn't enough for Mike. He had to do intricate stuff with buckets of water and huge boiling tubes from the chemistry lab. He had deeply hooded eyes and the kind of walk that just lopes along. How he'd ever got through an entrance interview was never quite clear.

He was a lovely bloke though. Asleep a lot of the time, often broke and really not very domesticated, but very nice all the same. Although, probably not the ideal housemate, if I'm being honest.

"Mike, have you been here all night?" I asked late one morning in the first term, having come downstairs to find him still hunched in front of the TV screen playing *Street Fighter Two*. After a while, and without turning around, he held up the back of a hand in greeting.

"I'll take that as a yes."

The hand became a thumbs-up. A lovely bloke maybe; but spending too much time with Mike could take its toll on anyone. Along with the other two we cycled around town and ate lots of packets of crisps in lots of different pubs. Eventually we found one where two halves cost less than a whole pint. This seemed like a good enough reason to spend most of our time there.

"Another three halves?"

"It's nearly home time. Let's make it a proper round."

"Six halves?"

"Just one for me."

"Five halves then."

"And see if they're giving away yesterday's sandwiches yet. What are they waiting for? They must be stale by now."

A university town can be a very boring place on a Saturday night, and it was only Tuesday afternoon. Somehow the landlord never seemed that pleased to see us, even though we were easily his most regular customers.

Eventually my tutors noticed that they couldn't actually remember seeing me that term. I was summoned to a low-ceilinged room with a polished tabletop and asked to explain where I'd been and, up to a point, who I was.

"Mr Ronay, your attendance record is very poor. The college takes an extremely dim view of this."

"I'm sorry."

"Do you have an explanation?"

"How do you mean exactly?"

"We mean maybe you could tell us where you've been all this time."

"Well, I have been a bit under the weather."

"Do you have a doctor's note? Have you registered with the college nurse?"

"And I've been doing lots of activities. College activities."

"I see. Anything specific?"

"Athletic activities. College sport."

"What precisely?"

"I've been playing a lot of football."

This was true. At the beginning of the year I'd been made captain of the college second XI. Our college didn't have much history of sporting success. It was too small and too quiet. I'd played the year before, once while I was still drunk from the night before. I think the outgoing captain thought it would be funny to put me in charge. It was that kind of team.

To everybody's surprise I began to take it seriously. This was the first time I'd ever captained a team. Perhaps more importantly, I had nothing else to do. Even more importantly, I'd reached a kind of crisis point in our house. It started when Mike first took up moving the furniture around. We used to come home and find him with the curtains drawn and surrounded on all sides by a wall of occasional tables and easy chairs. Often he'd be hunched in the middle of it all inside a sleeping bag; and always with a cloud of thin smoke clinging to the ceiling.

"I think he's building a kind of fort," Justin said one morning as we ate toast standing up in the hallway.

"It's quite sweet really."

"I suppose so."

"Mike," I said, sliding down next to a pile of heavy books that seemed to be squashing something flat in one of the armchairs surrounding him. "Are you, er, making some kind of hideout in here? And if you are, how long is it going to last?"

He stared at me for a while and then offered me what looked like a small flute. There was pale smoke emerging from the mouthpiece.

"No. Not right now. Thanks."

I soon got things moving with the football team. The college pitch was a large muddy field next to a dusty old pavilion. I decided to hold trials there for the start of the season.

"Why don't you just pick the same lot as last year?" Justin asked. "They're all still around."

"They lost every game last year."

"What are you going to do? Dig up hidden talent?"

"I don't know. I just want to do it properly."

My first masterstroke was managing to tempt Justin himself out of retirement. We needed a goalkeeper. Justin hadn't played for five years, but he was six foot four and he had telescopic arms. Over the season he turned out to be an almost unbreachable obstacle in our goal.

The team began to take shape. There was Tim, a pale first year, who turned up to every practice and then to every game whether he was playing or not. Tim was very quiet. At first I'd hardly noticed him. By the middle of the season he was one of my main men. We'd all come to rely on him. He had stamina, he kept running and he never complained. Sometimes it takes you a while even to realise you need things like that.

Big Paul was a fixture at centre half. Big Paul wasn't actually that big, but he had an air of authority about him. All season he glowered heroically in the middle of our defence. Away from the pitch he was a scientist in his fourth year with a gentle Yorkshire accent and glasses. On the field he remained committed to hoofing the ball as far as possible upfield while simultaneously screaming abuse at his team-mates, the linesmen and himself.

And towards the end of that first practice there was a pale kid with reddish hair and skinny legs, who turned out to be quick and skilful and tough too.

"What's your name?"

"Why? Are you going to put me in the team?"

He made little quotation marks in the air around the word "team".

"Don't make quotation marks in the air around my team. Where do you play?"

"Left wing. Right wing. Centre mid. Centre forward."

"Anywhere, then."

"I'm a modern footballer."

"So what is your name?"

"It's Lucien."

Lucien played in our first game of the season, next to me in midfield. None of us really knew what to expect. It hadn't occurred to me that we might actually win, but we did, Lucien scoring twice on a warm October afternoon. We walked off together at the end of the game in our scratchy purple shirts. The following week we won again in heavy autumn rain, and suddenly we had a proper team.

We kept winning more times than we lost. At the end of each week we waited for the league table to be printed and each time we'd still be floating around the top. The team was becoming something substantial in an empty year, an anchor in a place I'd never really felt I'd settle. By mid-season we were fit and strong. And there was no way I was going anywhere else that year, not with a promotion campaign still to be decided.

"We're third. St Anthony's keep winning. Forget about them. I think we need twelve points. Four wins."

"Halves all round?"

"Two halves for me."

"That makes four halves."

"I make it we can afford to lose twice," Lucien said.

"Let me see that. What if it's a complete tie?"

"They do it on goal difference."

"What if that's equal?"

"I don't know. Why are you asking me? Maybe they do it on how many Goths you've got in your team."

"I'm not a Goth. Goths are miserable. They wear eyeliner."

We were still in the top three when the days started getting warm again. Easter passed and we won a couple of games and then lost a couple more. It was a tense time. I had a five-second fight with an opposition midfielder who'd dived in at me as we both went for a loose ball. I came to my senses with my knees on his chest and a fist drawn back, wondering what I was supposed to do next.

"Sorry. I'm so sorry."

"My fault. No problem at all."

"That's very good of you."

"It's really nothing."

Eventually the season flattened out into one crucial final fixture. If we could beat St John's Hall we'd finish second and win promotion. I spent most of the week talking tactics with Justin. We picked a team, tore it up and picked it again. We checked the weather forecast. I spoke to each member of the team privately. Everybody knew what was required of them. Either that or they just nodded a lot and walked off quickly, stopping to check that I wasn't following them.

The game was an early kick-off on a bright May morning. We turned up early and sat in the sun behind one of the goals, watching as our team-mates appeared in the distance, a stream of tiny but familiar figures.

Alongside the usual faces we had a dark horse in our ranks. For the promotion decider I'd taken the decision to resurrect the career of Pete "Donkey" Davis, formerly talismanic mainstay of the college football scene. Now near the end of his fourth year, Pete was extremely unfit due to the overbalancing effect of his beer gut. Despite this he still had more skill than most and a powerful shot in both feet. My plan was to play him up front and tell him not to move from a narrow radius around the penalty area. It was a gamble, but today we needed something extraordinary.

We started like a runaway train, our momentum carrying us forward from the first whistle. The pitch was firm and dry and we passed the ball around, keeping it from the opposition. Ten minutes into the first half, I watched from twenty yards away as a pass from the left wing found Pete. He didn't have to move, just turn slowly, draw back his left foot and crash in a shot that swerved violently into the roof of the net. He looked as surprised as anybody. We mobbed him.

"Pete, you beauty."

"Where did that come from?"

"Steady, lads. Let me. Just get. My breath. Back."

We were still on our first wind. Moments later the ball was crossed in towards the near post. A tangle of legs sent it bouncing out to the edge of the area and into my path. I didn't break stride, hitting it hard and straight and just past the goal-keeper's grasp.

We knew it couldn't last. Soon we were defending for long periods, dropping deeper and deeper towards Justin in goal.

"Get out, reds."

"We can't get out."

"Just get out."

"Why does he keep telling us to get out? There's nowhere to get out to."

Just before half-time they pulled one back, a soft goal as a cross from the left crept in at the near post. The second half felt like a whole season on its own. Somehow we hung on to our lead. With Pete exhausted now and off the pitch, we chased and harried in every position. At the last Justin made an incredible save from a close-range header, thrusting up a hand to deflect the ball over the bar. And after an agonising last five minutes the referee blew for full time. All over the pitch we sank to the turf.

It was like a huge cloudburst, the disappearance of something dark and deadly that had been hanging over us. Before I knew it Justin had one of his huge arms around my neck. Pete "Donkey" Davis was punching the air. Above us the sky was totally empty, an impossible blue. And suddenly I loved every single one of us without exception, in a way I probably hadn't done since the days of Hanley Park and the Crofton Five-a-Side.

A scratch team with a faded purple kit, we'd been promoted, and the game had given me the single thing I'm still most proud of from my three years at university. Term ended a couple of months later in a blaze of hot weather. Before then there was time for the World Cup to come and go without Graham Taylor's England. At home we sat with the windows open in our living room and watched Brazil win the trophy from the middle of a sea of discarded lager cans.

Like Elton John at the height of his fame, football had saved me. That year it really did seem to be enough just to play twice a week and forget about everything else. I did play again the next season but it was never quite as big a deal. There were other things to do, like catching up on enough of the work I'd missed to scrape a decent degree. For now that could wait. I came home at the end of term feeling, for the first time, that I actually had something to leave behind.

I still see Justin now and then. He works for a big archi-
tects' firm, travelling the world helping to build railways.
Maybe it's part of always living out of a suitcase, but he still
reminds me of the lanky second-year student cycling around
looking for the cheapest half-pint of bitter in town.

Strange things happen to people over the years. Everybody
changes in one way or another. Right now Dan is doing the
hoovering. This seems unbelievable. Even more so, he's doing
it while I'm still asleep on the sofa. Although, to be fair, by now
I am definitely awake.

"What are you doing?"

"What? I can't hear you."

"Turn it off. Thanks."

"I'm cleaning up."

"I'm asleep."

"I can't help that. My parents are coming round today.
The place is a tip. Like you said, just pretend I'm not here. Life
goes on."

"Did I really say that?"

The hoover rumbles back into life, driving me out of the
room and into the kitchen.

Sometimes you wake up with the taste of last night's dinner
still in your mouth. It's a common experience, particularly if
you dine at Mr Slice. Today I've got more than just a taste.
There's definitely something crunchy still in there. I knew I
couldn't remember falling asleep last night. I wash it down
with a cup of tea from the pot. It's time to get myself sorted
out. I'm going to meet Laura this morning.

We're having showdown talks, although that sounds a bit too much like football. This is more like a clear-the-air discussion. Oh dear. I really am going to have to leave that kind of stuff behind today. This is one mid-morning brunch where football is definitely not on the menu.

There's a French café in Shepherd's Bush. You can tell it's a French café because it's called the French Café. It's got wooden floors and tables with white cloths that spill out on to the pavement. Accordion music wafts about. The waitresses are kitted-out in borderline French maid outfits. The men either mince around or brood in the corners. I manage to get there before Laura and settle at a table by the big window that fronts out on to the street. At least we'll have something to look at.

Laura appears in the doorway just as I'm ordering a drink. She's wearing a jacket I've not seen before and for some reason this makes me feel sad. She smiles when she sees me. You never do know how things are going to go until they're already happening. Pushing back a strand of hair, she kisses me on the cheek.

"Well here we are."

"Yes."

"I feel like we're on a date."

"I'm not a psychopath."

"What?"

"Isn't that what you worry about on dates?"

"I suppose so. But how do I know you're telling the truth? I mean, you look pretty normal. Actually, now you mention it ..."

"Thanks."

There's a long pause. Around us the late breakfast shift is changing guard as the lunch crowd arrive. Laura orders some food and we sit and watch through the window as the people pass on the street. A bus pulls up outside, a scroll of faces in profile. Neither of us feels like saying anything, but that's fine. Right now it feels as though it's enough just to be still here.

15
Lost

Sunday April 17th 2005
Farmingham United vs. Bolingbroke Athletic

Breakfast isn't just the best meal of the day. It's the best meal of the day by a mile. After a good breakfast there's usually only one thing that really hits the mark: more breakfast.

"Does anyone want some toast?" Kate asks.

"We shouldn't. We'll be off soon."

"It's no problem."

"Well, maybe just a piece. A couple if you're there already."

"Me too," Jerome says.

"I could fit some in," Dan admits.

"Yes please," Dave calls out from the end of the table where he's helping his son Louis get a few spoonfuls of green puree actually inside his mouth rather than just close to it.

"So that's eight pieces of toast then."

Breakfast at somebody else's house is even better. We're at Dave and Kate's place in Clapham, sitting around the kitchen table reading the newspapers and trying not to look at the clock on the wall, which must be getting pretty close to telling us it's our last call for getting on the road.

Outside it's a cold, clear morning. The sun is casting an orange glow across the top half of the room. Our kit bags are piled up in the hall, mixed in with the bikes and skateboards and mangled guns and cars. Family houses have a different kind of chaos. The flat may have been in a bit of a state when we left it this morning, but it's not the same. Family mess is warm mess. It doesn't really leave a mark.

"Where are we playing today?"

"Farnsworth. Farmingham. Somewhere like that."

"Keith said it's way out in the country."

On the floor, in between where Dan and I are sitting, little Jamie has started beating away at the roof of a plastic fire truck with a small wooden hammer.

"So where are we having lunch?" Dan asks.

"Are you serious?"

"If I'm driving us out to the middle of nowhere I need food."

"I did make some sandwiches," Dave shrugs.

Jerome is sitting on the other side of the table with his feet up on the side of Dave's chair, still zipped into his jacket.

"What kind of sandwiches?" he asks.

"Ham. Cheese."

"It isn't easy making a decent sandwich," Dan says. "You need the right combinations."

"Like what?"

"Something wet and something dry. Cheese is dry. Onion is wet. Ham and tomato is good. Two wet things or two dry things is no-go."

"Prawn mayonnaise and egg?"

"Too wet."

"Cheese and salami. Too dry."

"Exactly. People try and get around it by putting mayon-naise in everything."

"Then it's more like a burger."

"In America," Jerome points out, "a sandwich *is* a burger. That's what they call them."

"I don't want to break up the party. But shouldn't you all be going?"

Kate has reappeared. She pours herself a cup of coffee and quietly takes the wooden hammer out of Jamie's hand. For a moment this all seems a bit crazy. It's nine o'clock on a Sunday morning and we're going where? To do what? In a field? And we're getting there in a van? As usual this started off as Keith's idea.

"Is that your van then?" he'd said, the week after we'd lost away in Wimbledon. We'd just lost again to a team made up of set designers, actors and lighting directors. There was a rumour one of their players was a bloke who used to be in *The Bill*, but no one was quite sure which one.

"What *about* the van?" Dan asked.

"How about using it next week? We're away at God knows where in the country. We can all go down together, get a bit of team spirit going."

"I suppose so."

"And make sure most of us actually turn up this time."

Keith can get us to do most things at the moment. It's been a while since anyone mentioned the fact that we need to win a game somewhere along the line just to make it through to next season. It's like we've taken a collective vow of silence. But it's still hanging over us. Whatever else might be going on, it's there somewhere in the background.

This morning we've already picked up Jerome and now we're in the process of winkling Dave out of the house. That just leaves Keith and then we're off to meet the others down at the ground, wherever that might be. Keith's house is in the middle of a dinky white terrace on the fringes of a big super-market near the end of the motorway. It's quiet in the street, so quiet that we can hear his feet thumping down two flights of stairs to the front door.

"Give me a few minutes."

"We haven't got a few minutes."

"Just come inside for a sec."

Keith's living room is very neat. Everything looks polished and brand new.

"I can't believe he really lives here," Dan says, picking up a bronze lamp.

"You'd think he'd break everything. The door handles look like they'd come off in his fist."

"Right. Lads. Before we go, have a look at this."

Unshaven and still damp from the shower, Keith leads us through to the kitchen.

"What am I looking at?"

"The way forward. Fitness in your own front room."

A new gunmetal grey exercise bike is standing in the middle of the kitchen floor.

"I don't know, Keith. Exercise bikes," Dan says, sitting in the saddle.

"What's wrong with them?"

"It's a bit like the beginning of the end. You might as well get yourself a walk-in bath and a pair of those furry zip-up boots."

"The bloke said it strengthens your knees for football."

"Strengthens your arse for sitting down more like. Get yourself a proper bike. What's the point of cycling and not going anywhere?"

"Bollocks to the lot of you. Get off it. Go on, get out of my kitchen."

"We'd better, you know. We're properly late now."

The van seems to get bigger the more people you put in it. The engine growls as Dan spins the steering wheel with one hand and we crunch our way back out on to the main road. You get a good view in a van. You're up above the hedges and garden gates. If you're lucky you can get three people along the front seat. Dave and I win the race to ride shotgun next to Dan. Keith and Jerome have to make do with balancing on the wooden board in the back.

"Shall I risk it?" Dan wonders aloud, swinging over into the bus lane and through an orange light next to some shops. A woman with a dog watches us go past outside the newsagent's.

"Easy. These seats are useless," Jerome says from the back.

"Put your bag on the floor and lie down," Dan says. "It's much more comfortable."

There are a few cautious noises and the sound of a coat being unzipped.

"That is actually much better."

"There's nowhere left to fall over," Keith says. He's lying flat next to Jerome with his head on a towel.

"Do you want some privacy? We can close the back up."

It's still clear overhead, the sky fading to hazy white at the edges. It's cold outside, but not freezing, not February cold. Winter has started to move on but nothing has replaced it yet. The trees are still bare above the railings as we curve slowly around the edge of a cemetery and come to a halt at a small roundabout.

In my coat pocket I've got a carton of Ribena, a knee support, a disc with most of this week's work on it, and my phone. It's been turned on all morning. I switch it over to vibrate and put it back in my pocket. The last few weeks I haven't been able to shake the feeling of waiting for something to happen. It must be part of things still being a bit up in the air. It's different when everything's fine and settled. You don't check your emails every five minutes or look for the flashing light on the answerphone as soon as you get in through the door.

Not that I've got much to complain about. I'm still at Dan's place, but not for long I hope. Even my mum, of all people, has started giving me advice.

"How is Laura?" she asked on the phone yesterday, as though we'd just spent the last ten minutes talking about her. Which we hadn't.

"She's fine, I think."

"Good. I do like her."

She does too, which is a bonus of course these days. Funny how things like that change as you get older.

I saw Laura last week, just before she went off to a sales conference in Spain. She gets back today, come to think of it. In the course of things she as good as said she wants me to move in again. Only as good as, but that's still good. I thought I'd get this week out of the way before I tried for anything better. It's March. There really isn't that long to go now.

"Which way?" Dan asks as we stop at a four-way red light.

"Straight ahead. Bear left."

"What does bear left mean?"

"Straight left takes you into Asda. Bear left takes you to the motorway."

"I'm not sure that's right. Louis's nursery is down there."

"Dave, no offence," Jerome says from the back, "you've got a girl called Jamie and a boy called Louise. What's that about?"

"Louis. Not Louise. Watch what you're saying about my boy."

"It's fathers for justice. He's putting on his Batman suit," Keith says.

"Don't you think Batman's a weird kind of superhero," I say, as we slow to a crawl behind a coach. "He hasn't actually got any powers. Just a car and a fancy suit."

"There aren't many superheroes with actual superpowers," Dave says.

"What about the Hulk?"

"The Hulk isn't a superhero. He's just angry."

"A bit like you then, Keith," Jerome says.

"We could probably do with him today."

"Maybe he could get us to the motorway," Dan says,

changing the subject before Keith can get started. "Ah. Here we are. Motorway. Left-hand side."

Up ahead of us a police car makes a slow turn across four lanes and down a no-entry street, bringing the traffic to a halt. I slump lower in my seat. It doesn't seem possible that in less than an hour from now we'll be sprinting around a muddy field.

"Who else is playing today, Keith?"

"All the usual. Except Lucien's mate's in for Simon."

Simon had pulled out with a twisted knee after the defeat at Wimbledon two weeks ago. He hadn't seemed too sad about not being able to make it today.

"No place for the Hawk?"

"The Hawk is unavailable for selection. He's in Ibiza 'til after Easter."

"We should be bringing down two subs to these games. There should be thirteen of us. We should be turning people away," Dan says.

"We should, but we can't. How many teams do you see with subs? It's hard just getting eleven out. Nearly everyone's as old as us these days. There aren't the same amount of young players around like there used to be."

"Where are they all going?"

"Fuck knows. Too busy shoplifting and pissing in the lifts on my mum's estate."

"Keith, you're showing your age again."

"Yeah, well. Don't forget why we're all supposed to be taking this seriously. We're still right up against it."

There's a gloomy silence as Dan guides us out into the high-speed gridlock of the motorway. The van lurches forward, overtaking an ancient Mini and a Mercedes crawling along by the verge with its hazard lights on. A single white cloud has covered the sun, draining the colour out of the fields away to our left.

"You know something?" Dan says. "If you put your arm out of the window at this speed it feels like you're holding a breast in your hand."

"What?"

"Try it."

"I'm a married man," Dave says, winding down his window. "But you're right."

"Let me have a go," Jerome says, leaning across us and craning forward towards the window.

"Dan, you are a sick genius. Wait. Let me try something," he says, wriggling further out.

"No, don't do that."

Suddenly he's back inside again, gasping for breath after a failed attempt to force his whole head out of the window.

"That was never going to work."

"I had to try."

Up ahead of us a large sign has appeared with lots of names that don't sound very familiar. There's another, smaller sign with an exclamation mark on it.

"Keith, which exit do we take? I've never heard of Warncester."

"Was it on the directions?"

"What directions?"

"I don't know."

There's a brief pause while we take this in.

"Keith," Dan says. "You do have some directions, don't you?"

"I know where we're going. Framlingham or Farmlingham. I don't know the exact way."

"Why not?"

"It's your van. You're the driver."

"It's your team. You're the skipper."

"All right, all right. This isn't getting us anywhere," Dave interrupts.

"Yes it is," I say. "It's getting us to Warncester. Twenty miles now. Keith, are you sure about this Framlingham? It doesn't sound like a real place."

"All right, who's got the map? Let's have a proper look," Dave says.

"What map?"

"You must have a map?"

"This is my brother's van. He delivers sofas in South London. What would he need a map of Warncester for?"

I did have a feeling about today. People always say that with hindsight, but I really did. Then again I probably have a feeling about most days at the moment. I'm seeing omens everywhere. Although, being stuck in a van on the motorway with the clock ticking down and no map doesn't really qualify as an omen. It's a bit more than that.

In front of us something else is happening. Suddenly it's all getting a bit crowded out there. A brown car swerves across two lanes, hazard lights flashing.

"Oh dear. This is not good."

"Well. At least we've got some time to think."

The line of stationary cars stretches all the way around a slow bend in the road. The van shudders down through its gears as we slow to a crawl behind a red Ford Mondeo, which is suddenly just a few inches in front of us.

"Must be roadworks."

"It could be anything."

Traffic jams are always a bit of a shock. Standing still on the motorway feels all wrong. While you're whizzing along the world outside is just a backdrop. You're not really there at all. But then, suddenly, you are, and you're moving at five miles an hour.

"Look at this."

Dan takes his hands off the steering wheel and lifts his feet away from the pedals. The van keeps creeping forward in a straight line.

"Don't. That's weird."

The cars in the lane next to us gallop past briefly then stack up to a halt again. Heavy black tyre marks have scored the road into the central reservation, where the grass is surprisingly green. Time is starting to slip away. Keith lets out a deep breath and I can feel us all making a mental adjustment about what's going to happen for the rest of the day.

"Shall I call Charlie?" Dave says.

"Not yet. Give it a while."

"Something must be moving up there."

My own phone feels heavy in my pocket, a warm and secret thing. I glance down again, not really sure what I'm expecting. I think I just like looking. It feels like a pathway to somewhere else today.

"You know the thing about traffic?" I say.

"No. What's the thing?" Dan asks, not really listening.

"Traffic isn't really a problem. Everyone talks about it. But if they all stopped being bothered the whole problem would just disappear."

"You'd still be late."

"Twenty minutes. Half an hour. What's half an hour? You waste that long watching *Coronation Street*. Traffic is a state of mind."

"I did have this theory," Dan says. "If everyone in the country drove five yards closer to the car in front there'd be no more jams. You could do the maths."

We pass a grey car parked on the hard shoulder in a guilty puddle, steam still pouring from its bonnet. In the driver's seat a man is sitting reading a newspaper.

"We've got to make a decision," Keith says.

"It's your call, skipper."

"Keith, no offence, but why are you captain?" Jerome says. "How did that happen? Three years and nobody's ever told me."

"Don't get him started."

"Keith took control in controversial circumstances. It was a Keith d'état."

"The old skipper left and I took over. Simple as that."

"This bloke called Terry used to be captain," Dan says. "He started Bolingbroke. They used to live on Bolingbroke Road opposite the Bolingbroke Arms, Terry, Keith and the Hawk."

"What happened to Terry?"

"Good question. Dropped on his head when he was a baby probably. He was a bit of a nutter to be honest," Dan says, as a glimpse of open road appears in front of us.

"That's why we joined. People kept leaving," I say, remembering a very wet field, a cold flat in Brixton and a man called Terry who really did seem all right at first.

"Terry used to go mental and fight people. He was basically your nightmare captain. It all came to a head near the end of the season. He'd been getting worse and worse. Eventually he ended up chasing this poor kid down the road after a game, waving his boots above his head like he was going to kill him."

"And who was that poor kid?"

"Me," Keith admits. "It could have all ended there. But enough people wanted to carry on so we did."

"What happened to Terry?"

"He never came back. I think he was embarrassed. I saw him a couple of years ago. He doesn't play football any more. He works in television. He seemed really calm actually."

"Too calm."

"Yeah, well. Now, as your captain, I order you to get in the left-hand lane and stop at that services. I'm desperate for a piss."

"Good idea. We're not going anywhere out here."

Dan edges across two lanes and into a slip road that leads us through a funnel of hedgerows and into the haven of a motorway service station car park.

Outside the light has turned almost blue. There's a fresher wind out here and the gravel is wet, as though it's been raining recently. We shelter behind a small copse of trees and zip up our coats.

I have always quite liked motorway service stations. I know you're not supposed to. They're a guilty pleasure, an island of calm that never shuts just off a road that never stops moving. I like the fact that they're always the same. You always know where you are with a motorway service station.

"Lads, I'll see you in there," Keith says, breaking into a jog. We walk across slowly, feet crunching on the loose tarmac. A bird sings nearby as the automatic doors glide open and a warm cloud of air conditioning ripples over us.

"I'm starving," Jerome says.

"Me too. I shouldn't be but I am."

"Let's check out the shop."

Another thing about motorway service stations, it's impossible not to buy stuff. They have different kinds of food here. It's like being in an experimental chocolate laboratory. Dave buys a packet of giant Rolos. I'm torn between the white chocolate Twix and the frisbee-sized digestive biscuit.

"Check out the crisps," Dan says.

"Ringos. Discos. They've got everything. It's a crisp superstore."

There's something about crisps when you've got a bit of a

hangover. Most of the time, eating too many crisps makes me feel rough. With a hangover it's a different story. Something in the weird crisp chemicals does something else to the weird lager chemicals. And suddenly a packet of Chinese Lemon Chicken Sauce Nik-Naks is the only thing in the world that's going to make you feel better.

"Right, where is everyone?" Keith says, appearing with a pasty in his hand. We head out past the fast-food court, through the video arcade and into the cold air again with our plastic bags and steaming cups. Nobody says much as we head back towards the van. The only noise is Dan ripping open his tube of salt and vinegar mini poppadoms.

"Anyone?"

"Cheers."

There's one last pit stop on the way as we wait for Dan to fill up the van.

"Who said petrol smells nice?" Dave says. "I never got that."

"Maybe it used to smell better. Maybe they put different stuff in it now."

"They should go back to original flavour. It's like classic Coke. Never mess with a classic."

"Right then," Dan says as he slides back into the driver's seat and puts the key in the ignition. There's a long pause. We've been ignoring it, but it's pretty clear that someone has to do something. We're meant to be kicking off in about five minutes. We don't really know where we are or where we're going. And football is starting to feel like it's just not meant to happen.

"I should ring Charlie," Keith says at last.

"Yeah. You really should."

"They'll have seven."

"Seven's no good for a game."

"Eight maybe. I'll call him."

We all look out of the window as Keith holds his phone to his ear. There's almost a sigh of relief as he starts talking to Charlie's voicemail.

"Charlie, it's me, sorry we're not there, we've got stuck in traffic, it's getting on so start without us if you can, we'll be there soon as."

Keith switches off his phone and cracks open a can of Cherry Tango with the air of a man with something to celebrate.

"Well, there's nothing we can do now."

"Except drive. We're not turning back."

"No way. Let's see it through."

Calmer now, and with Dave giving Keith a turn up front, we pull out of the service station and join what has become a steady flow of cars, not quite a jam but a cautious half-speed. I almost feel like waving at the sign telling us to call again soon.

"You know," Dan says as we skirt around a small wood, "we really should have bought a map back there."

"Oh yeah."

"Oh well."

The landscape is more rural out here, the hillside on our right almost empty apart from a large barn. We watch the fence posts flicker past, heading into the sun, which is high enough to be just a rosy presence above the windscreen.

Another sign for Warncester appears, only this time we seem to have got further away from it.

"No mention of Farmingham."

"Or Farnsworth."

"There's a Framplington off at the next exit."

"Let's go there. I've never liked the sound of Warncester anyway."

We take the next fork off to our left, spiralling around towards a green field and a deserted crossroads.

"Right to Framplington."

"Sounds good to me."

"Okay," Jerome says, eating a sausage roll. "So we're going to a place we've never heard of just because it sounds a bit like another place we're not sure about."

"You know, Jerome, you're a real glass-half-empty kind of guy," Dave says.

"I've never understood that glass-half-empty thing," Dan says as we take a left over a bridge and head down a long road towards a church spire.

"That's what they say in the movies."

"It doesn't make any difference to what's actually in the glass though, does it? And at least if you think the glass is half empty you might actually try and fill it back up."

"I think we really are properly lost now."

We've found our way into a new housing estate, a grid of wide streets with identical semi-detached houses on either side. It doesn't even look as though anyone lives here yet.

"We've already come this way."

"We can't have."

"I've seen that gate before."

Eventually we come literally to the end of the road, the fresh tarmac petering out into a kind of builder's dump with piles of bright yellow sand and rubble.

"You know," Dave says as Dan turns the van around. "All this talk about next year and the team carrying on. I might not be able to play anyway."

"What?"

"Why not?" Keith asks.

"Well, the kids and everything. It just takes up too much time. It's nearly a whole day. And I can't recover like I used to. I'm knackered for half the week."

It's hard to argue with real things like kids and families and getting on in life. Nobody says anything for a while as we pull away and start to retrace our steps, but I think we all know Dave's got a pretty good point. We've been fighting against something that's probably inevitable in the end. Not that it means you have to stop just yet.

"Fair enough," Keith says. "Let's see how it goes. There's always the special guest appearance."

"He'll be wanting a testimonial next."

"Hey look. It's quite nice out here."

The housing estate has melted away into open country. A curtain of white mist is still clinging to the side of the hill down below us as we turn towards the sun again. The road is even narrower now, a single lane with stopping points. Cows stare as we rumble past. In the distance a column of grey smoke is rising, turning into cloud as it reaches the haze at the edge of the sky. We pass a farmhouse and then another and a cluster of cottages that turns into a small village.

"You know, it is lunchtime."

"There's definitely a pub. I saw a sign for it."

I glance across at Dan on one side and Keith on the other. "Shall we do it?"

"I think we'd better. As captain I officially declare us totally lost. Let's get into that pub."

This is just fine, really absolutely fine by me. I've just got a quick phone call to make. You never know. Air Espana might be running ahead of schedule.

"A pint of whatever local stuff they've got," I tell Dan. He heads for the bar as behind him Keith is pulling up chairs to the open fire. It looks like none of us is going anywhere in particular for a while yet.

16
Beginnings

Being twenty-four years old is either really good or really, really bad. In London it tends to veer between the two. There are places to go and people to meet. Your friends are always there for you. They may not be that much use, but they're definitely always there.

"I can see a table."

"It's fine. We can stand at the bar."

"But there's a whole empty table. Someone's just left."

"Why do we need to sit down? Three Stellas. It's gone now, anyway."

Dan turned and leaned back against the bar. I could see his point. It had taken us nearly ten minutes to squeeze our way from the door to somewhere we might be able to buy a drink. Next to me Simon had taken off his long coat and left it in a bundle on the floor.

"I told you coming out was a good idea. This place is heaving with women."

"Yeah, right. Sometimes I think good-looking girls only exist to torture me. I look at them and I feel physical pain."

"I'm sure the feeling's mutual," Dan said, taking a sip of

his drink. A pyramid of beer bottles was ferried through the crowd in front of us just as a sound like a chainsaw starting up began to emerge from the speakers above our heads.

Ever since we moved to Brixton the year before – the year after I'd left university – I'd walked past the Junction Box almost every day without being totally sure where the door was. It turned out the main room was a large vault inside a bricked-up railway arch. Tonight, its first under new management, there had been a queue right around the corner, almost level with the bus stop next to our flat on the other side of the road.

"Don't look. He's off already," Simon said, glancing over my shoulder.

Dan had started talking to the group of girls next to us. Pushed together by the swell of the crowd, he was actually standing right in the middle of the little circle they'd formed.

"We can't stay long," I said. "It's Richard's thing tonight."

"What thing?"

"Just a thing. I said we'd be there. He seemed to think it was important."

In the corner of the room a man wearing an anorak was hunched over a set of turntables. At ground level the music was just a noise, mixed in with the heat and smoke and the sound of the crowd. A glass smashed somewhere nearby as a crocodile of blokes in check shirts snaked its way across the dance floor.

"This is Linda and Suzie," Dan said. "These are my friends."

"Hi, are you a musician as well?"

"As well as what?"

"As well as your mate Dan."

"Oh. Yeah. I'm just as much of a musician as he is."

Linda and Suzie were both a little bit older than us. Suzie had red streaks in her blonde hair. They were wearing glitter on their faces that sparkled strangely in the light from the ceiling.

"Dan. Don't forget tomorrow."

"I won't forget. Relax. It's still early. Suzie was just telling me she met the drummer out of Blur in here."

"It was really funny. I was, like, you're, you know. And he was, like, you what? And I was, like, you what? And we were both, like, you what?"

Dan and I were doing something else tomorrow. Neither of us was really sure what to expect. I'd said we'd go and play football with a friend from work. His Sunday league team needed a couple of extra bodies. It seemed like a good idea at the time. Most things could seem like a pretty good idea back then.

I'd spent the last couple of years since college drifting from job to job. I'd taken my mediocre suit and old school shoes through merchant banks, insurance offices, a stockbroker and now a law firm.

My job was pretty simple. I was chief paper chaser on a huge case, stashed away in a room lined with files of photocopied documents. After my first few weeks I realised that nobody knew where anything was. All I had to do was look like I knew what I was doing and I was pretty much left alone.

Most of my day was spent sitting with my head over the desk drawer reading a folded up newspaper, ready to spring back up to attention the moment anybody appeared in the doorway. The rest of the time I chucked bits of paper at the bin. I developed a kind of bicycle kick, tossing the screwed-up memo in the air and volleying it across the room via a handspring off the side of my desk.

"You should come and play for us," the bloke from the office next door had said last Friday.

"Yeah, all right. Maybe I could bring my flatmate."

"Are you any good?"

"Oh yes. We're very, very good."

There's only ever one answer to that question. Actually we were both rubbish. Football had been one of the things to suffer recently, along with everything else connected to health, fitness and a well-regulated lifestyle. There had been the odd five-a-side and a handful of games every year for a pub team one of my brother's friends played for. Mostly life had been too chaotic. Weekends evaporated in a clamour of going out and lying in. Last Saturday I'd woken up on the sofa still in my suit and realised I hadn't actually taken my shoes off for three days.

"This place is a toilet," Dan shouted in my ear.

"It's not that bad."

"No, I mean it really is a toilet. Look at that wall over there. It used to be a gents."

"I love this track," Suzie cooed. "Let's go and dance."

"Only if we've got fags. I can't dance without a cigarette."

Dancing is a weird thing. Who really wants to dance? Most men will do it, but only if certain conditions are met. The music must not be disco. It's got to be after closing time. Ideally some kind of prop will be available, like a drink or, in extreme cases, a circle of your mates jumping up and down. And there must be at least some chance that dancing will lead to sex.

The last condition is the most important. Without it any kind of dancing is just a non-starter. Take away any possibility of sex and men will drink instead.

"This place is brilliant," Linda said, giving me an ultraviolet smile. She had a soft edge to the way she talked, like she wasn't totally convinced you were actually listening, but then she wasn't really sure she cared that much anyway.

"Listen," I said, leaning over towards Dan and Suzie. "We're going to a party. Do you want to come?"

"What sort of party?"

"A house party. Down the road."

"Sounds good. Let me get my friends."

Simon had joined the band of serious-looking men nodding their heads around the figure in the corner. He was standing very still, about three rows back from the front. We picked him up on the way out, along with Linda, Suzie and Daisy. I'd seen Daisy earlier dancing on a little stage and wearing a sparkly tiara. She still had it on her head as we squeezed past a line of bulky men in leather coats and out into the freezing wind.

"Remind me where we're going and why," Simon said as we turned back towards Brixton.

"To a party. Don't keep asking me about it."

We walked through the gloom under the broken streetlamp and beneath the bridge where the pigeon crap had made the pavement slippery. I zipped my jacket up to the chin. It was my only decent coat, bought with a whole month's salary last year when the heating in our place in Elephant and Castle had packed up. None of us mentioned the flat as we walked past it. Somehow the place didn't really create the right kind of mood.

A group of kids outside the Greek grocer's stared at us while I tried to remember the way to Richard's. Kids seemed to be getting much younger and much tougher. How were they managing to do that exactly? Our breath steamed the air as the cars hissed past, the street wet from the freezing drizzle.

I knew Richard from university. Our friendship had been resuscitated and kept alive by his moving to the same part of London. He and Dan didn't really get on. They both worked in the City, but while Dan drank lager and wore a bomber jacket with a reflective badge that made him look like an electrician, Richard drank wine and wore brogues and had even been seen smoking cigars. He was a friend, though. And you can forgive a friend almost anything. Even cigars.

"This way," I said, pointing down a side street. "No, left. Oh shit. What are they doing?"

"Come on then," Daisy was shouting

"You want some, do you?" Suzie joined in, laughing loudly.

The two girls had started waving at the gang of kids outside the supermarket. The kids stared back, not really sure what to do as Daisy pretended to chase after them across the street. Dan had strategically disappeared behind a phone box.

"Yeah, great, let's keep walking shall we?"

Simon trudged gloomily ahead, while I trudged gloomily behind. There was definitely something wrong with me. In the last few years it felt like I'd met quite a few Suzies and Daisies. They just kept coming. And they were obviously having a pretty good time of things. It was me I wasn't quite so sure about.

"We've been walking for hours. Where is this place?"

"Let's get another drink. The Caspian's still open. One more can't hurt."

So we bundled in through mirrored double doors and sprawled around a table ringed with leather cubes and a huge, creaking beanbag that smelt like an ashtray. As I gripped the table and fell into a sitting position I realised that, yes, we really were much drunker than I'd thought.

"Dan. Tomorrow. Don't forget."

"Yeah, yeah."

"Yeah, yeah what?"

"Football," he said. "What's this team called anyway?"

"Boglingbroke? Something like that."

"Wake me up before you go go. I'll be there."

The night seemed to disappear after that. A few hours later morning came creeping under the curtains like a burglar jimmying his way in through the bedroom window. Something fairly serious had happened inside my head. Not nuclear, not terminal, but bad enough. I was on my back and I was in bed. That would have to do for now.

The flat was made up of four rooms arranged around a narrow corridor in the bowels of a terraced house. We had a window at the front and a window at the back. My room was a damp cell in the middle. Waking up there was like finding yourself hidden inside a giant mouldy cheese. A cat from the family upstairs used to come in, but in the end we had to keep it locked out. Dan kept waking up with it curled up on his face.

The digital clock said 08.20. I thought about this until it said 08.45. On the face of it there was no reason why I couldn't get up, drag Dan out of bed, load us both into the clattery old Renault that my brother's girlfriend's dad had sold me, and get us down to Richmond in time for kick-off.

So this was what I decided to do. Pausing only to roast my ankles in front of the blow heater by my bed, I beat a path into Dan's room.

"Yeah. I know."

"We've got ten minutes. Are you in here on your own?"

"Why shouldn't I be?"

"No reason. I thought that Suzie ..."

"Yeah, well you thought wrong. Anyway, it's football. I'm a professional."

The game was at Ham in Richmond. I'd driven past before on the way out of London and seen the pitches. As we weaved through the green fringes off the main road bridle paths loomed up out of the rain and early morning walkers wandered past in green wellies.

"Last night was a bit of a disaster then," Dan said from almost inside the hot air blower on the dashboard.

It was true. Richard's party hadn't really worked out. The first inkling I'd had that things weren't going to plan came when he opened the front door. There wasn't any sound of loud music playing. Nobody was milling around in the hallway or sitting on the stairs.

"Er. Come in."

"Cheers, Rich, this is Linda, Suzie, Daisy."

"Hi."

"Hi-ya."

Inside it looked as though everyone had already left. There was just one small group still sitting around the dinner table. They even seemed a bit surprised as we came bowling in, Daisy wearing her tiara, Simon in his long coat and horrible hat with earflaps and Dan with Suzie now almost completely draped across him. We'd had time to get some take-out beers and a bottle from the Greek grocer's so it couldn't have been that.

In the hall Richard ushered me off to one side. He had red wine stains on his teeth and he was wearing something that looked like a waistcoat.

"What do you call this?"

"It's a bit crap but you can't get anything else in the CheapaSava."

"Not the wine. You turning up now. And bringing all these people."

"Rich, to be honest it looks like it's a good job I did. A bit quiet, isn't it? Where is everyone?"

"Everyone we invited for dinner has been here for the last four hours. Apart from you."

In the living room Simon was leafing through Richard's records. Linda and Daisy were trying to stop laughing long enough to dance. Dan and Suzie were sitting in a tangle of legs on the sofa.

"Hello. I'm Barney," I said, sitting down at the table. No

one said much in return. There were a few mumbled greetings. After a while a girl with dark brown hair started giggling. I was pretty grateful for it at the time. But she stopped when nobody else joined in.

"He could have said it was a dinner party," Dan said, after I'd stopped to ask directions to Ham House from a man in a deerstalker hat. "It's still a party anyway. Just with dinner."

"No, it's the other way round. It's dinner with a little bit of party."

"He's not old enough to have dinner parties."

"He's the same age as us."

"And when was the last time we had a dinner party?"

"Never. It looks like we won't be going to any for a while either."

At the end of a long gravel track we found the pitches. I parked the car next to a low brick changing room. The rain had found yet another second wind.

"What's this bloke called again?"

"Dave. The captain's called Terry."

"Right then. We'd better get out there."

"I suppose we had."

"Right then."

Grabbing our plastic bags with boots and shin pads we ducked across the car park, through the nearest door and straight into a ten-foot cube containing eleven other men. Our new team-mates. For a second everybody just stared. In among the unfamiliar faces I spotted Dave. He shifted over as we sat down next to him.

"Morning. Just in time. You'll fit right in."

Gradually the chat, the fiddling with kit and all the usual changing-room sounds started up again. Dave introduced us to Terry. Stocky and dark, with half an inch of stubble, Terry could have almost been mistaken for a proper footballer. This was despite the pair of grey nylon socks he was wearing over his shin pads and the fact that as the door closed I realised there were no lights or windows in the changing room. In the darkness we rooted in the kit bag for shorts and shirts.

"Lads, you'll have to start sub."

"No worries. Who are we playing?"

"William Cobbett House."

"Are they any good?"

"They beat us 9–0 last year."

"Yeah, but are they any good?"

"Ha ha. Very funny."

The field at Ham was surrounded by a hedgerow on two sides and some tennis courts on another. As we trotted across in single file, collars turned up against the rain, my boots started to soak up water and expand back into shape like rehydrated prunes.

The pitch was in a slight dip and the surface had a sweaty, bog-like feel. Some practice balls were being knocked around between the white shirts. I hung around on the fringes next to Dan, wondering whether my legs would still know how to kick a football.

It was strange just being outside in such a wide open space. The sky looked huge and ridiculously bright. I've always liked rain. It puts a roof on the world. Today it seemed to be connecting us with a great inverted lake above our heads. Feeling my feet start to freeze I eased into a rusty jog, slaloming from side to side. Going to the Junction Box, meeting Suzie and Daisy, turning up at Richard's dinner party mob-handed all seemed a very long way away.

"Mate, you look like you had a few too many last night."

"Er yeah. Maybe."

I was standing next to a large man with a round cheery face. He was slightly overweight, just enough to make him look like a chubby schoolboy.

"Nev, by the way." He held out a hand.

"I'm Barney. This is Dan."

"Lovely," he grinned. "About time we had some fresh blood."

The team had just started to separate into a distinct set of faces. There was Terry, the skipper. Out here he looked wiry and intense. He was watching in silence as our very tall goalkeeper, Lars, rolled up a trouser leg to show him a bandage on his knee. A small, bearded middle-aged man walked past wearing the number nine shirt.

"Oh my God. It's Tom Finney," Dan muttered.

"He's probably fitter than both of us."

"Hello. I'm Bob."

"Bob. Hi."

By now the opposition had lined up in formation, a collection of figures in red shirts and white shorts. Terry came across to where we were standing on the touchline.

"You'll get a half, don't worry."

"That's fine. A half is great."

"There is one thing. You'll hate me for this, but can you run the line? There's a flag over there."

The game kicked off in driving rain, the kind of rain that comes in horizontal waves, like having a bucket of water thrown in your face. We started badly. For five minutes the game refused to stray from within a short radius of the penalty area. Everything was being slowly dragged down into the plughole of the Bolingbroke goal.

"Out! Get out!"

"MAN ON! SEND IT NOW!"

"Jesus. What have we got ourselves into?"

"It looks like it's about our level. Ref! That's a foul."

"You're the linesman. Wave your flag."

Soon the opposition scored. There was a sense of anti-climax about it. A shot from distance leapt out of a puddle and bobbled over the line before the keeper Lars could claw it back.

For the rest of the half the game stayed compressed into the same small space. In attack Bob twisted and turned without getting anywhere near the ball. There was almost nothing to raise the flag for. After twenty minutes my jacket had reached a point of total saturation and I could feel a trickle of rain running down the back of my neck. As we waited for the ball to be fetched from some spiky bushes I noticed Dan was laughing to himself.

"What's so funny?"

"Just thinking about last night. The dinner party."

"They looked really surprised."

"Yeah," he said. "Poor old Dicky. Sitting there with his mates from work and that Laura he's been trying to impress for about the last year."

"She was the one who laughed at me. Right."

"Oi! Fucking clear it. No! For fuck's sake."

Terry scampered after the ball on the right-hand side as Nev fell over heavily in the full back position. Before long the opposition had scored twice more, the last a trickle over the line after a slow-motion melee six yards out.

"Well. It's good to be out," Dan said. He had a scarf wrapped around his face as well as a soaking woolly hat on his head.

"This is nice actually."

"We must be still drunk."

Half-time arrived suddenly. Walking across stiffly, we gathered on the edge of the circle of Bolingbroke players. For a few moments there was silence as water bottles were ripped open and bags unzipped.

"Right, well you don't need me to tell you that was an absolute fucking disgrace," Terry said quietly.

There was steam actually coming off the top of his head and a gleam in his eyes that hadn't been there at the start of the day. Looks were exchanged. Bob sighed.

"Terry, don't start."

"You'll know when I've started."

"Yeah well don't."

The break passed in an uncomfortable silence, broken only

by the sound of the rain. A water bottle sloshed. Somebody fiddled with a boot. Nev spoke into a mobile phone off to one side while Bob wrapped himself up in a beige raincoat with lots of flaps. Dave came and stood next to us. He looked cold and very pale.

"Lads, before we go back out I need a volunteer to come off."

"Leave it fifteen if you want," I suggested.

"You sure?"

"Oh yeah. No worries. No problem."

"What did you say that for?" Dan said as we headed over to the far side. It had stopped raining and the grass had begun to steam slightly. The air smelt fruity and rotten.

"I don't know. Just being polite."

The second half began as the first had finished, with the white shirts immediately pushed back deep into defence.

"No. No. Fucking no."

The team swearer had turned out to be Charlie, a skinny midfielder with a slightly wild look about him whenever he got near the ball. At least he looked like he was really trying. Come to think of it, perhaps he was trying a little bit too much.

In the distance a man had appeared by the entrance to the field. He was wearing a cap and holding a golf umbrella. We watched him approach, a coloured speck getting larger as he wound his way around the tennis courts. He was dark and stocky with a heavy brow and deep-set eyes. He nodded at us as he reached the touchline.

"GET UP HIS ARSE!! Ref, for Christ sake!"

"It's 3–0 to the reds," I told him.

"Jesus."

We watched in silence for a while, my flag still drooping on its pole. The ball bobbled about the middle of the pitch, sticking in the mud occasionally

"REF, FOR FUCK'S SAKE!" the man with the umbrella shouted. "I'm Keith by the way. Oh look. Here he goes."

Charlie was just starting to pick himself up after a heavy tackle near the centre circle. There was a loud splash as Terry stamped his foot in a puddle. Despite being at least a head taller, the red-shirted player in front of him had already started to retreat, but not quickly enough. With the speed of a scampering chimpanzee, Terry was on his back, toppling him over into the mud. Near to us Dave shook his head wearily as the referee scampered across and stood over the wrestling figures, peeping on his whistle.

"That boy is a nutter," Keith said.

"Yeah. Looks like it."

"An hour gone. He's like clockwork."

By now Terry was being raised from the ground in a bear hug by Nev. Even as he was carried from the field, taking a weary-looking Bob with him, he started giving us the "get warmed up" sign.

"You two. Get out there quick before he can send me off."

With twenty minutes left Dan and I squelched on to the field together for our first taste of action in a Bolingbroke shirt. The sky was clearing slightly now. A few patches of milky blue had appeared. My feet still completely frozen, I lined up with the rest of the back four.

Unexpectedly my first touch was a miracle: a volleyed pass straight over the top of two players and into Charlie's stride. For a moment I was stunned. Where had that come from? Somewhere buried within the memory bank; a reflex from the reaches of a lifetime spent playing football. Or maybe it was just a fluke.

I spent the next five minutes in a daze. It's easy to forget how exhausting playing football is. In a vague quest for fitness I'd been going out running occasionally. Running is all about finding a balance between legs and lungs. It's a truce between breathlessness and pain. As long as you don't lose the rhythm you can just about keep going.

Football has no rhythm at all. There's no way to cushion your body from it. Sprints are followed by more sprints, by leaps and pauses and shouts. The only thing that can prepare you for football is more football. Even at our level, at a quarter speed in a team that's already 3–0 down, there's nowhere to hide.

Despite this Dan seemed to slot into midfield without breaking stride. A couple of passes, a neat turn and suddenly he was back, just the same as ever. With both of us down by the corner flag I put in my first tackle, carrying the ball away in a swamp of topsoil and legs.

"COMMITMENT! LET'S HAVE SOME MORE OF THAT!" Keith shouted as I untangled myself, but I was already up and after the play.

And for a few minutes I lost myself completely in a game of football again. Nothing else existed outside of the ball, the white lines, and the geography of friend and foe, as I chased and stumbled, and kept running towards where Nev and Charlie spent most of the last ten minutes grappling with a ginger-haired winger.

The final whistle broke the spell. It seemed like a very short half in the end. Cold suddenly and very wet, we trudged back with Keith towards the low brick buildings in the distance by Ham House.

"So do you play, normally?" I asked him.

"Yeah. Not this week. I'm suspended," Keith said.

"What for?"

"Fighting."

"What happened to the other bloke?"

"He's over there. Still captain of the team."

In the changing room I realised that every piece of clothing I'd brought was soaked. My hand was bleeding, my right knee had started to throb and a deep cut had opened up under the caked mud on my shin. I was too tired to talk much to my new team-mates who, after thirty minutes of football, already seemed like people I'd been on a very long journey with. The afternoon ended on a strange note, taking a hot shower with twenty-two other men in complete darkness. Nobody talked much.

On the way home the rain had started to fall again. It battered the windscreen as we sat in traffic off Putney High Street, lulled by the sleepy Sunday lunchtime gridlock.

"That was all right," Dan said.

"Almost seems a shame to go home."

"You know what we could do?"

"What? What could we do?"

"Turn left here."

"But we're going home."

"Home is a state of mind. Home is also really cold. Let's face it, home smells of mould."

Ten minutes later we were back in the Junction Box, almost in the exact same spot at the bar we'd been standing a few hours before. A hunched figure in the corner, possibly even the same hunched figure from last night, was playing music that sounded a bit like the air lock in our hot water system. A few crumpled figures grazed at the bar, or sat at the tables furthest from the windows.

"Right. A couple of pick-me-ups," Dan said.

"I'm dehydrated. Nothing serious. Just lager."

"Lager for sir. An excellent choice."

Two hours later the bar had started to fill up. There was a crowd around us now and, almost unnoticed, the music had started to get louder again. The light was fading outside. Before long it was almost as though the events separating last night and this evening – football, dinner parties, waking up – had all been a strange interruption.

"This is what we do from now on," Dan said above the noise in the room. "Go out, get up, play football, go out. Best of everything."

"You've got to keep in shape."

"Exactly. We owe it to ourselves."

Things haven't always been as easy as they seemed that Sunday. But for us it was definitely something. It was definitely a start.

17
Endings

Sunday May 15th 2005
Bolingbroke Athletic vs. Racing Balham

In football endings always happen in sunshine. All those make-or-break games and relegation deciders, they're always played at this time of year. The mud and freezing rain is just preparation. Sometimes seeing things right through to the finish can be the hardest part of all.

It's light outside when I wake up. It's May now and already football has started to fade into the shadows. In London a week of hot weather changes the landscape. On Thursday afternoon for a couple of hours it felt like July, and by the end of the week Shepherd's Bush had begun to give off the hot, sweet smell of a city that's struggling to breathe.

Today we're at home to Racing Balham. It's the final game on the fixture list. It's also the last time, for a while, I'll have to set the alarm on a Sunday, slide out from under the duvet and tiptoe downstairs to the kitchen, leaving Laura still sound asleep on her side of the bed.

We've played twice more since the game at Framlingham or wherever it was supposed to be before we got stuck somewhere else. Both times we lost: narrowly in Holland Park to a team of twenty-year-olds; and then heavily to a pub team with a coach who ran along the touchline shouting instructions for the whole ninety minutes.

I think we always knew it would come down to today. Not because of fate or destiny or anything like that. Just because the last game of the season is the only one we haven't had a chance to lose yet. The equation is the same. One measly victory and Bolingbroke Athletic get to stay alive for another season. And still, somehow, I have to admit I'm not totally, completely switched on today. Football seems to be happening to someone who looks like me, sounds like me, and might even be me. It just doesn't really feel like me.

By nine o'clock the sky has turned a deep powdery blue. On the Embankment the trees are thickening and the sun flashes on the tall windows in the streets around Battersea, flushing out the Sunday morning mist that has lingered all winter. I pick up Dan in Clapham. Red-eyed, he shrugs his bag into the boot.

"You look really rough."

"Yeah. Thanks. It takes a lot of work."

He's wearing a blue rugby shirt with white paint stains across the front, the arms scissored off at the elbows, and he's got a pair of ancient flip-flops on his feet.

"What did you do last night?"

"I went out with my cousin. A quick drink. A bit of dinner. Home by closing time."

"Sounds harmless."

"A party in Oval. A bottle of Bell's from the all-night offie. Some girl called Karen. Cousin disappears. I end up walking the streets at four in the morning looking for a cash machine to buy fags."

"We really need to have a word about your pre-match routine."

Today it feels as though we're being drawn towards Halfmarshes by some invisible force. Gravity drags us across the one-way system, through green lights and over empty junctions. Every now and then you've just got to let things happen. Soon today will be gone and over and fading away into the past, but not before it's had its say.

We pull into the little lane down to the ground and I see Keith's car and Nev's jeep parked in the shade. The gravel path, the dripping tap, the green fence that's been looking as though it's about to fall over for the last five years. Nothing has changed. The sound of Dan closing the boot makes me jump. We're all here early today. The door to the changing room has been propped open, letting in the warm air. It feels like the end of term, the countdown to six weeks of summer holiday.

"All right, lads."

"Keith."

Keith is sitting in his vest by the door, his head disappearing into his shoulders as he scratches his chin. Nev strolls in naked from the showers and arranges himself in the corner next to the hot water pipes. Charlie is tapping his feet softly and whistling between his teeth.

"Well, you all look up for it. Just stay like that 'til the opposition turn up," Dan says, putting his bag down.

"I've been here for half an hour," Keith says. "What do you want? Press-ups?"

To be honest Keith doesn't really look himself this morning. Some people you take for granted. Good humour, endless energy, unstoppable enthusiasm, in the end everything has its limits. The kit bag lies beached and emptied on the tiles, its guts spilt out and divvied up for the last time this year. Opposite me Jerome wraps tape around the top of his socks.

"Before we go out," Charlie announces, clearing his throat. He blushes slightly as we all go quiet. "In case we don't get a chance, I just wanted to say thanks to Keith. Thanks for organising everything. And for keeping us going."

"Well done, skipper."

"Cheers, Keith."

"Go on the Keith."

There's a clatter of applause round the room and some whistling from Jerome. Simon puts a long arm around Keith's shoulders.

"All right. All right. Fuck off. We're not finished yet. We've still got a game to play. Now. No. Stay there. Lads, a word about today. Oi! Shut it."

"Yes, sir."

"Like I said, we can win this. I want us to close down space from the start. Defend from the front. And the back."

"Defend from the front? So where do we attack from?"

"From the front. And also … from the back."

"So we defend and attack from the front and from the back."

"Exactly."

"Brilliant. Why didn't we think of that before?"

There's a murmur around the room. Simon goes back to fiddling with a boot. Jerome stretches the back of his legs against the wall. Keith's tactics may be muddled. His game plan may have holes in it. But he is right about one thing. Forget the form guide. Forget the goals against tally and the points per game ratio. Forget the fact that Bob has decided to play in glasses today. There is still something to play for.

As we run out together into milky sunlight even the kit feels warm on our backs. There is a reason why I'm not really with it this morning.

This is how it happened.

Things have been different with Laura for the last couple of weeks. Different, as in much better. At first we both made a big effort. Then, after a few days, it stopped feeling like it was any kind of effort at all. She's seemed happy too, even a bit distracted. Last Saturday we stayed in bed until three o'clock in the afternoon. I don't think Laura's ever slept that late in her life.

So everything's been better these last few weeks. Take Friday night. We went to the theatre.

"There's something I really want to see at the South Bank," Laura said.

"Er. All right then."

"It's based on the lost diaries of Hitler's butler. It's supposed to be very powerful."

"Fine," I agreed, not saying any of the things I might have said, not pretending to fall asleep and not even beginning to question my own sanity. "I'll get the tickets."

We met at Waterloo and weaved our way through the people running for trains, and across two lanes of taxis to the river. It was already dark by the time we got there. The reflection of the buildings on the far side reached all the way across to the concrete bank down below us. We found our seats and settled in just as the lights dimmed and marching band music began to play over the PA system.

The best thing about the theatre is going to the bar at the interval. It's the sudden mad rush for the door and the way everybody knocks back their drinks like it's 10.55 on a Friday night. But then, any kind of alcohol tastes good after an hour and a quarter of small talk in the bunker.

"Do you want another one?"

Laura hadn't touched her glass of wine.

"No, it's all right."

"Are you sure? We've still got five minutes."

"Have mine if you want."

"All right. I will."

It did feel good to be doing something out of the ordinary. Even if the best bit was turning out to be the one most like what we did the rest of the time.

"We don't have to go back in, you know," I said.

"What do you mean?"

"We've seen half of it. I can fill in the rest. The main thing is, everyone dies."

So we went for a walk instead. It wasn't exactly what I had in mind, but it was absolutely fine with me.

Outside the river was a deep chocolate brown. There were

lights in the trees along the footpath, leading us in a broken line towards the wharves and high-rises of the City. A boat passed with people dancing on deck and under a bridge an old man with white hair was playing the violin. After a while we'd pretty much forgotten about everything but the cold air and the sound of our shoes clacking on the concrete.

"You don't think we should have stayed to the end, do you?" Laura asked.

"No. Not at all. To be honest I've never been that into the theatre."

"Why not?"

"I don't know. The seats are too small. There's always someone behind you laughing really loudly just to show they get it."

"You poor thing."

"Maybe it's the actors. I used to think they were taught to speak like that."

"Like what?"

"Like they know the whole room's listening to them. That was before I actually met any actors in real life. It doesn't really matter though. Other people like it."

"Philistine."

"How can I be a philistine? I don't even know what a philistine is."

A jogger appeared up ahead with a flashing light on a strap around his head. We let him pass in silence.

"You know," Laura said. "There was something I wanted to talk about."

"Oh God, what? If it's the grill I'm going to clean it tomorrow. It's next on my list."

"What list? No."

"Toilet seat?"

"The toilet seat is not a problem. I am capable of lowering it myself."

"Cool. So what's up?"

"I'm pregnant."

As she spoke she was looking straight at me with a funny little smile I hadn't seen before. Then suddenly she was crying and I had my arm around her shoulders and her cheek pressed into my neck, wet with tears, although she actually seemed very happy and not sad at all.

"I've been waiting for the right moment."

"When could it not be right?"

"I don't know. Over breakfast."

"So are you all right then?"

"Yes," she said. "I'm fine."

And she really did look it. We started walking again, slower now, with both her hands in my coat pocket. And right there on the riverside a strange, powerful feeling came over me, and two words just kept popping into my head, two little words that seemed to sum up exactly how I felt right at that moment. Oh fuck.

Oh *fuck*.

We got a taxi all the way home. Laura laughed and said not to be silly she was fine and I went along with it, not telling her I felt a bit too faint to walk myself. On Saturday morning I watched her wake up. Then I watched her eat breakfast and get dressed. I watched her fiddle with her window boxes. I watched her so closely that after a while she said, "Can you please stop watching me?"

There are some things nothing can prepare you for. I told Dan the news on the phone.

"How long has it been?"

"Three months. She knew for a while. She just wanted to be sure."

"You must be really happy."

"I'm still pinching myself. But yeah. It's not that simple. But yeah."

Dan laughed.

"What's funny?"

"It's a good job at least one of you actually knows what you're doing."

I'm thinking about that as we take our positions for our final game, the one we've been talking about off and on for the last six months. As we stretch and bend and jog on the spot I feel a hand on my shoulder.

"One more time," Simon says.

"Go on then."

We push each other in the chest a bit and then he gives me a couple of high fives.

"Are you all right?" he asks.

"Yeah."

"You sure?"

"Kind of. I'll tell you later."

In the distance the opposition are already in place. I take a last look around the white shirts: Lars in goal; Nev, Keith and Dave, a familiar sight in defence; Jerome and Lucien wide on the wings; Charlie and Dan ready to fight for the middle. Up front Simon looming over Bob on the edge of the centre circle.

The game kicks off in weak sunshine and the first ten minutes are just a blur. The ball keeps going out into the bushes on the far side of the field. It's too hot for this. It's too bright. My shirt feels sticky and tight around the neck. When the ball does come to me I give it to someone else quickly.

"Come on, whites. Switched on."

"Keep it going. This is good."

But it's not good. It's a bit like we're asleep. Lucien takes a whole minute just standing over a free kick. The keeper at the far end chases the ball towards the cricket pitch and places it for a goal kick and I feel like I'm counting off the seconds.

Soon the red shirts have their first proper attack. They're a better team than they looked before kick-off. Keith wins a tackle and gets up with the ball still at his feet. Moments later Dan has a shot from a long way out that fades away wide of the goal. The sun makes me squint as I follow the arc of the ball, and I'm thinking about the summer and about Laura and something makes me remember the games we used to play at school, when football was just something that happened to you after lunch, but the game still took you over immediately so that nothing existed outside the lines of the pitch.

In front of me Jerome wins a corner and back by the halfway line I hear the shouts. I'm almost involved, almost disappointed as Nev sends a rebound wide from close in, the ball making a slapping sound as it hits his thigh.

After a shapeless forty minutes the red shirts finally score. It's a great goal, a curling shot into the top corner by a stocky midfielder with white boots. I watch from behind as the ball hits the space beyond Lars's glove and I feel like clapping.

"Come on, whites. Unlucky."

"Straight back in, boys," Keith shouts.

The half-time whistle blows and we troop across to the touchline. We're all breathing hard. Nev has turned a deep shade of red and the back of Dave's shirt is damp with sweat. We sit in a wide circle, socks rolled down, even in the middle of everything enjoying the sun and the soft grass.

"Have a drink, lads," Keith says. "Get some water on board."

"Here," Dan passes me a plastic bottle with a cloudy liquid in it.

"What's this?"

"Hangover cure. You get it in those outdoor rock-climbing shops. I don't know what it is. But it makes you feel better."

The liquid tastes salty and it fizzes slightly. He's right, though. It's like a tonic.

"So. What's going on then?"

"I don't know. That's a very good question. What is going on?"

Dan shrugs. "You know, for someone who's the happiest man alive, you don't seem very happy."

"Yeah. Well. It's not that easy."

"What's not easy?"

"The whole thing. I do feel happy. If I really think about it I feel so happy I can't cope almost. It goes beyond that."

"Into panic."

"Panic. And fear. Right now I suppose I just feel pleased for Laura."

"I wondered when I was going to hear anything about her," Dan says. We're both lying flat on the grass. Above us the sky is so blue you can't even focus on it.

"Oh she's fine. She's cool. She's really well actually. To be honest this whole pregnancy thing has made we wish I'd spent as much time as possible with her before it all happened."

"Right. I mean I'd just assumed you were, you know, sticking it out together."

"Of course we are. We might even get married, not that it seems like such a big deal any more."

"It's a bit of a coincidence really," Dan says, stretching a hand up in front of his face. "I split up with Bobby last week."

"Really? Oh shit. I'm sorry."

"Don't pretend you liked her much."

"I did sort of like her. She was a good laugh. Did *you* actually like her?"

"I must have a bit. Occasional guest sex appearances isn't much of a relationship though. I'm going to find myself a twenty-year-old. Settle down behind a white picket fence somewhere."

"Er ... you are kidding?"

"When I'm fifty. So how long has Laura known?"

"She found out for sure a week ago. Actually it happened

when Michael was staying. Probably the same night I kicked him out."

"You want to get a DNA test done on that kid."

"Piss off."

"Oi, lads," Keith shouts out. "Two minutes. Get warm again."

"I'm boiling as it is," someone mutters.

"Anyway," Dan says, sitting up. "People have kids. It happens all the time. We are nearly thirty. Someone's got to do it."

And watching the white shirts start to stir I get a picture of something different. It's the thought of still being able to do all this, doing it all over again with someone else. I can hold the coats. I can shout from the touchline. I can be embarrassing.

"I can live out my own failed ambitions through the next generation."

"Exactly. Give you something to do when you're older and fatter. You need to start being a bit more pleased about this. Hey, Si. Has he even told you?"

"Told me what?"

"Laura's up the duff."

"No. You're kidding."

"We only just found out," I say.

"That is great news." Simon punches me on the arm, then gives me a kind of half-hug, then punches me on the arm again.

"What's this?" Keith asks.

"Laura's pregnant."

"No way? Fucking brilliant." He slaps Simon on the back and then grabs me in a bear hug. "Poor girl, she's far too good for you. When's it due?"

"November, I suppose."

"He supposes."

"What's going on?"

"His missus is pregnant. We're having a Bolingbroke baby."

"Mate. Absolutely fantastic."

Now I'm being hugged by Nev. Bob shakes my hand warmly. Even Jerome seems bowled over by the whole thing. And it's like a valve has opened somewhere. Something in the sun, in the way Keith slaps the back of my neck with the palm of his hand, makes me think of hot water rushing into a bath.

"Right," Keith says. "Now. Time to go back out, lads. We've got forty-five minutes. You've all seen this lot. They're good but they're not that good. I know it's hot. I know we're tired. But we've got nothing to lose here."

The opposition are already standing in formation. As we kick off it feels as though the sun is right above our heads. A breeze has shouldered its way through the haze, just enough to keep the heat off our backs. I go to fetch a loose ball from the bushes and the air tastes sweet.

We're kicking down towards the trees and railway line now. The shadows on the grass are sharp as we move forward and the pitch is lush where just a month ago it was piled and rutted mud. It feels springy underfoot. I dive in at a red shirt as he's about to cross the ball, feeling the ground reach up to break my fall.

Dan passes the ball out to Charlie and gets it back. It feels easy. We're not going anywhere, just enjoying ourselves, running through what we've done so many times before. It feels like we won't be completely denied today, as Jerome skips inside his man and puts in a cross that Simon catches perfectly with his forehead.

The ball curves away, isolated against the blue, striking metal and bouncing down with a loud clank. There's a smack as it hits the ground and then a fizz as it spins into the folds of the net. I let the feeling, the arc of the ball into the net, settle over me, a moment of clarity preserved, and then we're running after Simon and back towards our own goal.

That's as good as it gets. Time seems to be moving quickly today. With the score at 1–1 the final whistle is a gentle sound. It's like a release. We've done all we can. There's some applause and handshakes, hugs between the two teams. We sit in the centre circle as the red shirts troop off. Next to me Keith looks resigned.

"Well done, lads. Well done, everyone."

"Is that it then?"

He smiles weakly. "Barring some minor miracle. Yes. That is it."

"What do you mean?"

"We're still bottom of the table."

"No, the miracle bit."

"I don't know. Maybe someone else won't register for next year. Maybe some teams will go bust or break up. Maybe we can blag it. We'll see."

"We'll still have something," Dave says. "Five-a-sides. Friendlies."

"Darts. Snooker."

"Bowls," Jerome suggests. "Who's up for bowls? Nev?"

"Great. Let's do it."

"Bolingbroke bowls it is then."

In the changing room the steam from the showers curls out of the window and into the sunlight. Nev wobbles past, dripping like a big pink dog. There are some things I won't miss about football. We're all louder than usual today. I can't really hear what anyone's saying, it's just noise and laughter and the sound of Keith shouting in someone's ear. None of us feels like being the first to leave.

"What are you doing this afternoon?" Dan says, his hair still damp as we stand up.

"I don't know. Hanging around. You?"

"I thought I might clean the flat up. Sort out the spare room. Go shopping."

"Really?"

"But then I decided to go to the Windmill instead. The beer garden should be open."

"Sounds good. Maybe we'll come and join you."

Outside we sit in the shade on the cracked wooden bench. Dan kicks off his flip-flops. In front of us the long field stretches away down to the fences at the far end, the empty goals half-turned, looking like a doorway into more green space.

Simon sits down next to me. Keith joins us on the other side and we sit watching the cars leave one by one, getting smaller as they curve away along the gravel lane before disappearing out of sight behind the trees. Somewhere in the pale blue an aeroplane fades out of earshot and a slow silence descends all around us, one I hadn't even noticed was missing.